Microsoft®
WINDOWS NT®
WORKSTATION
VERSION 4.0

Step by Step

Other titles in the *Step by Step* series:

For Microsoft Windows 95

Microsoft Access for Windows 95 Step by Step

Microsoft Access/Visual Basic for Windows 95 Step by Step

Microsoft Exchange Step by Step

Microsoft Excel for Windows 95 Step by Step

Microsoft Excel/Visual Basic for Windows 95 Step by Step

Microsoft Office 95 Integration Step by Step

Microsoft PowerPoint for Windows 95 Step by Step

Microsoft Project for Windows 95 Step by Step

Microsoft Visual Basic 4 Step by Step

Microsoft Windows 95 Step by Step

Microsoft Word for Windows 95 Step by Step

Microsoft Works for Windows 95 Step by Step

More Microsoft Windows 95 Step by Step

Upgrading to Microsoft Windows 95 Step by Step

For Microsoft Windows 3.1

Microsoft Access 2 for Windows Step by Step

Microsoft Excel 5 for Windows Step by Step

Microsoft Excel 5 Visual Basic for Applications Step by Step, for Windows

Microsoft Visual FoxPro 3 for Windows Step by Step

Microsoft Mail for Windows Step by Step, versions 3.0b and later

Microsoft Office for Windows Step by Step, version 4

Microsoft PowerPoint 4 for Windows Step by Step

Microsoft Project 4 for Windows Step by Step

Microsoft Word 6 for Windows Step by Step

Microsoft Works 3 for Windows Step by Step

^{Microsoft®} WINDOWS NT® WORKSTATION VERSION 4.0

Step by Step

Catapult

Microsoft Press

PUBLISHED BY
Microsoft Press
A Division of Microsoft Corporation
One Microsoft Way
Redmond, Washington 98052-6399

Library of Congress Cataloging-in-Publication Data
Microsoft Windows NT workstation version 4.0 step by step / Catapult, Inc.
     p.   cm.
    Includes index.
    ISBN 1-57231-225-4
    1. Microsoft Windows NT.   2. Operating systems (Computers)
3. Microcomputer workstations.   I. Catapult, Inc.
QA76.76.063M52476 1996
005.4'469--dc20
                                                   96-31376
                                                    CIP

Printed and bound in the United States of America.

2 3 4 5 6 7 8 9 RM-T 1 0 9 8 7 6

Distributed to the book trade in Canada by Macmillan of Canada, a division of Canada
Publishing Corporation.

A CIP catalogue record for this book is available from the British Library.

Microsoft Press books are available through booksellers and distributors worldwide. For
further information about international editions, contact your local Microsoft Corporation office. Or contact Microsoft Press International directly at fax (206) 936-7329.

For Catapult, Inc.
Managing Editor: Diana Stiles
Project Editor: Armelle O'Neal
Production/Layout: Jeanne K. Hunt, Editor;
Carolyn Thornley
Writer: Mary Hutson

For Microsoft Press
Acquisitions Editor: Casey D. Doyle
Project Editor: Laura Sackerman

Catapult, Inc. & Microsoft Press

Microsoft Windows NT Workstation version 4.0 Step by Step has been created by the professional trainers and writers at Catapult, Inc., to the exacting standards you've come to expect from Microsoft Press. Together, we are pleased to present this self-paced training guide, which you can use individually or as part of a class.

Catapult, Inc. is a software training company with years of experience in PC and Macintosh instruction. Catapult's exclusive Performance-Based Training system is available in Catapult training centers across North America and at customer sites. Based on the principles of adult learning, Performance-Based Training ensures that students leave the classroom with confidence and the ability to apply skills to real-world scenarios. *Microsoft Windows NT Workstation version 4.0 Step by Step* incorporates Catapult's training expertise to ensure that you'll receive the maximum return on your training time. You'll focus on the skills that can increase your productivity the most while working at your own pace and convenience.

Microsoft Press is the publishing division of Microsoft Corporation. The leading publisher of information about Microsoft products and services, Microsoft Press is dedicated to providing the highest quality computer books and multimedia training and reference tools that make using Microsoft software easier, more enjoyable, and more productive.

Table of Contents

Table of Contents

Table of Contents

*Quick*Look Guide

Getting help,
see Lesson 2, page 34

Managing windows on the Desktop,
see Lesson 1, page 15

Opening recently used documents,
see Lesson 2, page 30

Using menus, commands, and dialog boxes,
see Lesson 1, page 9

Manipulating windows with the taskbar,
see Lesson 2, page 31

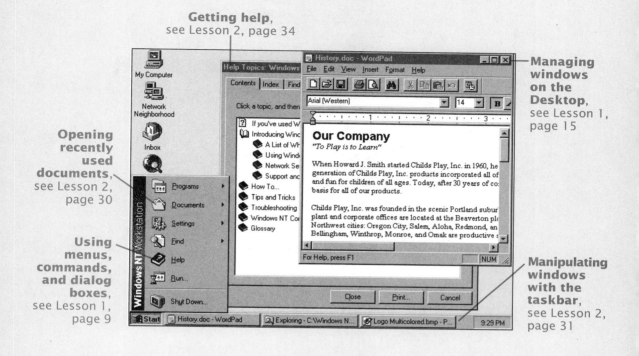

Using shortcuts,
see Lesson 3, page 48

Customizing your mouse,
see Lesson 3, page 55

Customizing your Start menu,
see Lesson 3, page 44

Customizing your display,
see Lesson 3, page 56

Customizing your programs,
see Lesson 3, page 45

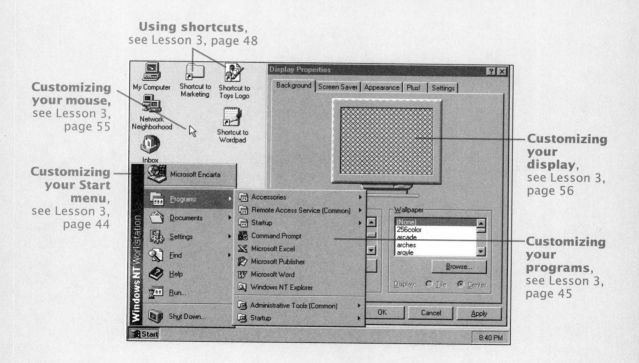

Drawing pictures, see Lesson 5, page 88

Sharing information between different programs, see Lesson 6, page 115

Using MS-DOS–based programs, see Lesson 6, page 107

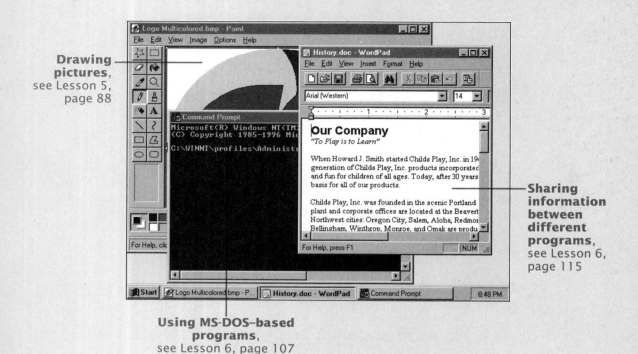

Writing documents, see Lesson 4, page 72

Switching among multiple open programs, see Lesson 6, page 112

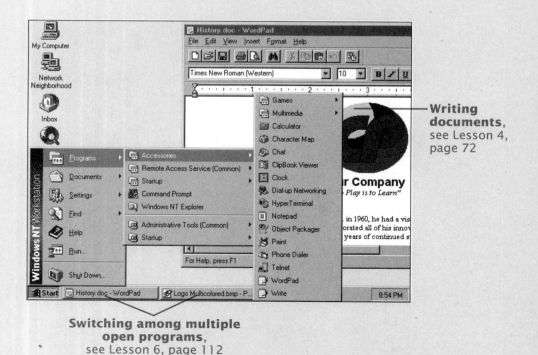

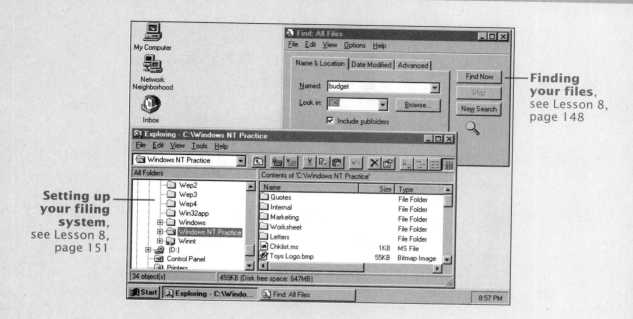

Finding your files, see Lesson 8, page 148

Setting up your filing system, see Lesson 8, page 151

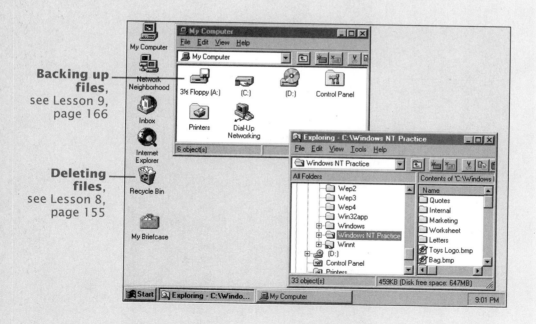

Backing up files, see Lesson 9, page 166

Deleting files, see Lesson 8, page 155

*Quick*Look Guide

Working on a network,
see Lesson 7, page 131

Sending and receiving messages with Microsoft Exchange,
see Lesson 7, page 140

Transporting files between computers with My Briefcase,
see Lesson 10, page 183

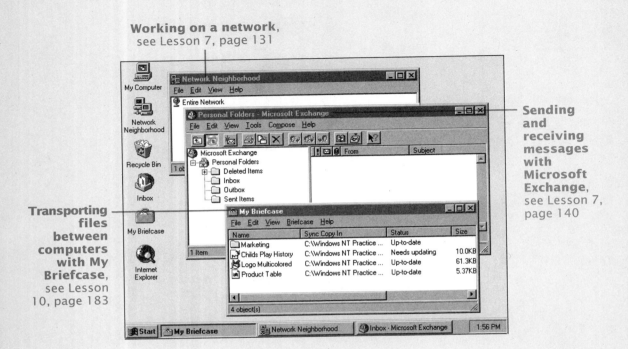

Calling another computer with HyperTerminal,
see Lesson 11, page 203

Exploring the Internet,
see Lesson 11, page 197

Calling another computer with Dial-Up Networking,
see Lesson 10, page 190

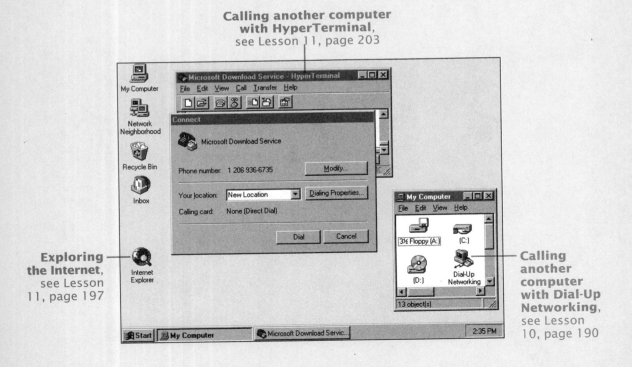

Finding Your Best Starting Point

Microsoft Windows NT is a powerful operating system that you can use to efficiently set, customize, and manage your computer work environment. *Microsoft Windows NT Workstation version 4.0 Step by Step* shows you how to use Microsoft Windows NT to streamline your work and increase your productivity. With this book, you can learn Microsoft Windows NT at your own pace and at your own convenience, or you can use it in a classroom setting.

 IMPORTANT   This book is intended for use with the Microsoft Windows NT Workstation version 4.0 operating system with a Default setup. If a specific installable component is required for a lesson, installation instructions will be given directly in the lesson or you will be referred to the appropriate documentation. To determine what software you are running, you can check the software documentation, the installation disk labels, or the exterior product packaging.

Finding Your Best Starting Point in This Book

This book is designed for readers learning Microsoft Windows NT for the first time, for experienced readers who want to learn and use the new features in Microsoft Windows NT version 4.0, and for people switching operating systems. Use the following table to determine your best path through the book.

If you are	Follow these steps

New...

to computers

to graphical environments

to Windows NT

1 Install the practice files as described in "Installing and Using the Practice Files," the next chapter in this book.

2 Become acquainted with the Windows NT operating system and how to use the Windows NT online Help system by working through Lessons 1 and 2.

3 Learn basic skills for using Windows NT by working sequentially through the rest of the lessons.

If you are	Follow these steps

Upgrading...

from Windows 3.x

from Windows 95

from Windows NT 3.5x

1 Learn about the new features in this version of the program that are covered in this book by reading through the following section, "New Features in Windows NT version 4.0."

2 Install the practice files as described in "Installing and Using the Practice Files," the next chapter in this book.

3 Complete the lessons that cover the topics you need. To locate general topics, refer to the Table of Contents and QuickLook Guide. To locate information on a specific topic, refer to the Index.

If you are	Follow these steps

Switching...

from UNIX

from OS/2

from any other operating system

1 Become acquainted with the Windows NT operating system and how to use the Windows NT online Help by working through Lessons 1 and 2.

2 Install the practice files as described in "Installing and Using the Practice Files," the next chapter in this book.

3 Learn basic skills for using Windows NT by working sequentially through Lessons 1 through 3. Then, you can work through Lessons 4 through 11 in any order.

If you are	Follow these steps
Referencing... this book after working through the lessons	**1** Refer to the Index to locate information on specific topics. Refer to the Table of Contents and *Quick*Look Guide to locate information on general topics. **2** Read the Lesson Summary at the end of each lesson for a brief review of the major tasks in the lesson. The Lesson Summary topics are listed in the order they are presented in the lesson.

New Features in Windows NT Workstation Version 4.0

The following table lists the major new features in Microsoft Windows NT version 4.0 that are covered in this book. The table shows the lesson in which you can learn about each feature.

To	See
Explore the new Windows NT interface.	Lesson 1
Use Help.	Lesson 2
Start programs and documents with the Start button.	Lesson 2
Manage and manipulate your open windows with the window controls and the taskbar.	Lesson 2
Customize your menus and Desktop.	Lesson 3
Create shortcuts to programs, folders, and documents.	Lesson 3
Give long filenames to Windows NT files.	Lesson 4
Create and edit text documents with the WordPad accessory.	Lesson 4
Create and edit graphics with the Paint accessory.	Lesson 5
Open and use new Windows NT accessories, including new Desktop tools and system utilities.	Lesson 6
Find and run Windows NT-based programs.	Lesson 6
Start MS-DOS Command mode and run MS-DOS-based programs.	Lesson 6
Make information available on a network.	Lesson 7
Create, send, and receive e-mail messages with Microsoft Exchange.	Lesson 7
Share files and folders with others on a network using Network Neighborhood.	Lesson 7

To	See
Organize your files and folders using My Computer and Windows NT Explorer.	Lesson 8
Move, copy, and rename files and folders using new Windows NT techniques.	Lesson 8
Delete and retrieve files and folders using Recycle Bin.	Lesson 8
Back up important information.	Lesson 9
Synchronize files that are duplicated on different computers with My Briefcase.	Lesson 10
Work remotely using telecommunication.	Lesson 10
Connect to other computers through telephone lines by using Dial-Up Networking or HyperTerminal.	Lesson 11

 NOTE   We invite you to visit the Microsoft Press World Wide Web site at http://www.microsoft.com/mspress. You'll find descriptions for all of our books, information about ordering titles, notice of special features and events, additional content for Microsoft Press books, and much more. You can also find out the latest in software developments and news from Microsoft Corporation by visiting site http://www.microsoft.com. To install a shortcut to the Microsoft Press Web page from the practice disk, see the next chapter, "Installing and Using the Practice Files." We look forward to your visit on the Web!

Installing and Using the Practice Files

The disk included in the back of this book contains practice files that you'll use as you work through the exercises in the lessons. For example, in the lesson that teaches you how to create graphics using Paint, you'll open a practice file, and then display and edit a graphic. Using the practice files means that you don't have to spend time creating the samples used in the lessons yourself—instead, you can get right to work learning the concepts in the lessons. Because the practice files simulate tasks you would encounter in a typical business setting, you can easily transfer what you learn from this book to your own work environment.

IMPORTANT   Before you break the seal on the practice disk package, be sure that this book matches your version of the software. This book is designed for use with the Microsoft Windows NT version 4.0 operating system. (If you need some help installing the software, see Appendix A.) If your operating system is not compatible with this book, a Step by Step book that matches your software is probably available. Many of the Step by Step titles are listed on the second page of this book. If the book you want isn't listed, please visit our World Wide Web site at http://www.microsoft.com/mspress/ or call 1-800-MSPRESS for more information.

Install the practice files on your hard disk

Follow these steps to copy the practice files to your computer's hard disk so that you can use them with the lessons.

1 If your computer isn't already on, turn it on now. You might see a dialog box asking for your username and password. Type the requested information in the appropriate boxes, and then click OK. If you don't know your username or password, contact your system administrator. If you see the Welcome dialog box, click the Close button.

2 Remove the disk from the package at the back of this book.

3 Insert the disk in drive A or drive B of your computer.

4 On the taskbar at the bottom of your screen, click the Start button, and then click Run.

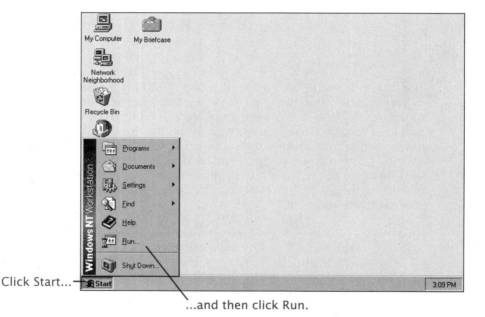

Click Start...

...and then click Run.

5 In the Run dialog box, type **a:setup** (or **b:setup** if the disk is in drive B) in the Open box. Do not add spaces anywhere.

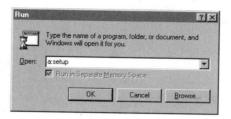

6 Click OK, and then follow the directions on the screen.

The Setup program window appears with recommended options preselected for you. For best results in using the practice files with this book, accept the recommendations made by the program.

7 When the files have been copied, remove the disk from your computer and replace it in the envelope at the back of the book.

A folder called Windows NT Practice has been created on your hard disk.

NOTE In addition to installing the practice files, the Setup program created a shortcut to the Microsoft Press World Wide Web site on your Desktop. If you're computer is set up to connect to the Internet, you can double-click the shortcut to visit the Microsoft Press Web site. You can also connect to the Web site directly at http://www.microsoft.com/mspress

Using the Practice Files

Each lesson in this book explains when and how to use one or more of the practice files for that lesson. When it's time to use a practice file in a lesson, the book will list instructions on how to open the file. The lessons in this book are built around a scenario that simulates a real work environment, so you can easily apply the skills you learn to your own work. For the scenario in this book, imagine that you're an employee at Childs Play, Inc., a toy manufacturing company. All the computers at Childs Play have been updated to Windows NT version 4.0. You must now learn how to use the new operating system. You'll first learn how to get around Windows NT, and then you'll use Windows NT in your work.

In Part 1, "Learning the Basics," you'll begin to get familiar with Windows NT. You'll get more practice on how to use the mouse, and you'll give commands to Windows NT using menus and dialog boxes, locate files, and use the taskbar to manage your windows. You'll learn how to get help when you need it. You'll also customize your Windows NT environment, just as you might decorate and arrange items in your office to enhance your efficiency and comfort.

After you're oriented and comfortable with Windows NT, you'll be ready to get to work. In Part 2, "Using Windows NT Accessories and Tools to Get Your Work Done," you'll start working with some of the Windows NT programs. You'll create documents with the built-in accessories called WordPad and Paint, and you'll see how you can work with multiple Windows NT–based programs, as well as MS-DOS–based programs.

As you go through this book, you'll be creating files. You'll find that as you do more and more of your own work, you'll be creating still more files. Windows NT makes it easy to organize your files for quick access. In Part 3, "Sharing, Organizing and Backing Up Information," you'll learn how to set up a filing system, manage your files and disk drives, as well as find and back up files stored on your computer.

You might also need to exchange information with others outside your company. In Part 4, "Getting Connected,"you'll learn how to share your files in your workgroup or with people outside your company, on a network or across the telephone lines.

Conventions Used in This Book

It will save you time using this book if you understand the way instructions, keys to press, and so on are shown before starting the lessons. Please take a moment to read the following list, which also points out helpful features of the book that you might want to use.

Procedural Conventions

- Hands-on exercises that you are to follow are given in numbered lists of steps (1, 2, and so on). An arrowhead bullet (▶) indicates an exercise with only one step.
- Text that you are to type appears in **bold lowercase**.

Keyboard Conventions

- A plus sign (+) between two key names means that you must press those keys at the same time. For example, "Press ALT+TAB" means that you hold down the ALT key while you press TAB.
- Procedures generally emphasize use of the mouse rather than the keyboard. However, you can always choose menu commands with the keyboard by pressing the ALT key to activate the menu bar. Then, sequentially press the keys that correspond to the highlighted or underlined letter of the menu name, and then the command name. For some commands, you can also press a key combination listed on the right side of the menu.

Note Conventions

- Notes or Tips that appear either in the text or in the left margin provide additional information or alternative methods for a step.

- Notes labeled "Important" alert you to essential information that you should check before continuing with the lesson.

- Notes labeled "Troubleshooting" alert you to possible error messages or computer difficulties, and provide solutions.

Other Features of This Book

- You can learn about options or techniques that build on what you learned in a lesson by trying the optional "One Step Further" exercise at the end of the lesson.

- You can get a quick reminder of how to do the tasks you learned by reading the Lesson Summary at the end of a lesson.

- You can quickly determine what online Help topics are available for additional information by referring to the Help topics listed at the end of each lesson. The Help system provides a complete online reference to Microsoft Windows NT. To learn more about online Help, see the "Getting Help with Windows NT" section in Lesson 2.

- You can practice the major skills presented in the lessons by working through the Review & Practice sections at the end of each part. These sections offer challenges that reinforce what you have learned and demonstrate new ways you can apply your newly acquired skills.

- In Appendix A, "Installing Windows NT Workstation version 4.0," are instructions on preparing for and installing Windows NT on your computer.

- In Appendix B, "Matching the Exercises," you can review the options used in this book to get the results you see in the illustrations. Refer to this section of the book if your screen does not match the illustrations or if you get unexpected results as you work through the exercises.

- In Appendix C, "Working with Other Operating Systems," you can get information on working with previous Windows, Windows NT, or MS-DOS programs.

Learning the Basics

Working with Desktop Tools

Estimated time
30 min.

In this lesson you will learn how to:

- Control window elements.
- Use commands and menus.
- Specify options and properties in dialog boxes.
- Move and size a window.

When you start a new job, one of the first things you need to do is become familiar with your work environment and the tools available to you.

In this lesson, you'll familiarize yourself with the Microsoft Windows NT screen and be introduced to the basic tools available to manage your work environment. You will also get acquainted with the different screen elements and learn how to use the mouse to control your computer.

Getting to Know Your Desktop

When you start Windows NT for the first time, you see a few items displayed, such as the My Computer icon in the upper-left corner, and the *Start button* in the lower-left corner. The Windows NT screen is also called the *Desktop*. Just like on an actual desk, the items that are on your Desktop vary depending on your current tasks and projects. The contents of your Desktop can change as your work changes.

If your screen looks different from this illustration, see Appendix B, "Matching the Exercises."

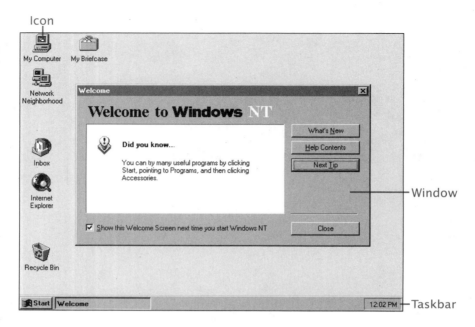

The rectangular bar that runs horizontally across the bottom of your screen is called the *taskbar*. The taskbar includes the Start button, the starting point of your work on the computer. The taskbar also shows the current time. When you start working, you'll see other buttons listed on the taskbar which show you the names of the windows currently open on your Desktop.

The named pictures along the left side of your screen are *icons*. Icons graphically represent items you use while working or playing in Windows NT. For example, the My Computer icon represents all the programs, documents, and other resources available to your computer system.

Controlling Windows NT with the Mouse

You use the mouse to select icons, buttons, or other elements on your Windows NT Desktop. Using the mouse is intuitive and provides a direct way to select, move and activate screen elements.

There are four basic mouse actions to help you carry out different functions, such as displaying a menu, choosing a command, or opening a file. The following table summarizes these mouse actions.

For this action	Do this
Point	Move the mouse pointer to a specific location on the screen by moving the mouse.
Click	Press and release a mouse button.

For this action	Do this
Double-click	Press and release the mouse button twice in rapid succession.
Drag	Point to an item on the Desktop, hold down the mouse button, move the mouse to a different location, and then release the mouse button.

Most of the time, the mouse pointer looks like an arrow. However, the mouse pointer can change shape, depending on where it is placed on the screen or what command you have chosen.

With Windows NT, you use both the left and the right mouse buttons. If you use a three-button mouse, you can ignore the middle button. The primary mouse button is initially set as the left mouse button and is used for most mouse actions. The secondary mouse button, the one often used to access shortcuts or perform special actions, is initially set as the right mouse button.

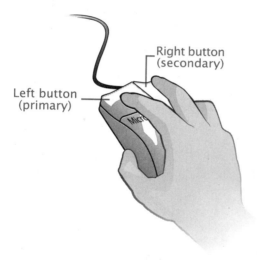

Right button
(secondary)

Left button
(primary)

 NOTE Throughout this book, any reference to the mouse button refers to the left mouse button, unless otherwise specified.

Making Desktop Choices with the Mouse

If you have set up your practice files, you used the mouse to move the pointer on the Desktop and click commands. In the next two exercises, you'll learn more about selecting Desktop elements using both the left and right mouse buttons.

Select Desktop objects with the mouse

In this exercise, you practice pointing and clicking using the mouse, and observe how these actions affect the screen elements.

1 If your computer isn't already on, turn it on now.

2 Press CTRL+ALT+DELETE to log on.

3 Type your password if you're using one, and then press ENTER.

If you see the Welcome dialog box, click the Close button.

Close

4 Move the mouse until the tip of the pointer is positioned on the My Computer icon.

5 Click the mouse button once.

The My Computer icon changes color, indicating that it is selected for further action.

6 Pull the mouse toward you until the tip of the pointer is positioned on the My Briefcase icon, which is displayed on the left side of your Desktop.

7 Click the mouse button once.

The My Briefcase icon changes color, indicating that it is now the selected icon.

Pointer

8 Move the mouse pointer over the Start button in the lower-left corner of the Desktop, and then click the mouse button once.

The Start menu opens as shown in the following illustration.

9 Move the mouse pointer to an empty area of the Desktop, away from the Start menu, and then click the mouse button once.

The Start menu closes.

10 Move the mouse pointer until the tip of the arrow touches the top edge of the taskbar.

The mouse pointer changes to a two-headed arrow.

11   Move the mouse pointer to any empty area on the Desktop.

The mouse pointer changes back to the standard arrow.

Open shortcut menus with the mouse

In certain areas on your Desktop, you can click the right mouse button to open a *shortcut menu*, which lists commands that directly relate to the action you are performing. In this exercise, you see how the commands available on shortcut menus vary depending on where you click.

1   Point to an empty area of the Desktop, and click the right mouse button once.

A shortcut menu appears, listing shortcut commands for the Desktop.

2   Point to the My Computer icon, and click the right mouse button once.

A shortcut menu appears, listing shortcut commands applicable to the items stored in My Computer.

3   Use the left mouse button to click an empty area of the Desktop.

The shortcut menu closes.

Performing Actions by Double-Clicking with the Mouse

You can perform some actions quickly by *double-clicking* items located on your Desktop. You double-click to instantly open an object, such as an icon or a file.

Open programs or files by double-clicking icons

1   Place the mouse pointer on the My Computer icon and double-click it.

    The My Computer window appears. The name of the window also appears as a button on the taskbar.

If the Welcome To The Windows Briefcase wizard appears, click Finish.

2   Double-click the My Briefcase icon.

    The My Briefcase window opens, and its name appears as a button on the taskbar.

3   Double-click the Recycle Bin icon.

    The Recycle Bin window opens, and its name appears as a button on the taskbar.

Moving Items by Dragging with the Mouse

You can move and resize objects on your Desktop by *dragging* with the mouse. For example, you can drag to move a window or an icon, or to change the size of a window.

Move Desktop objects by dragging with the mouse

1   Position the mouse pointer on the words "Recycle Bin" at the top of the Recycle Bin window.

2   Hold down the mouse button and drag the window about one inch to the right, then release the mouse button.

    The Recycle Bin window moves to the right.

3   Place the mouse pointer on the Recycle Bin icon.

4   Hold down the mouse button and drag the icon to the right of the My Briefcase icon, then release the mouse button.

    The Recycle Bin icon now appears at the bottom of the screen.

5   Drag the Recycle Bin icon upward to its original location.

Telling Windows NT What To Do

Windows NT is a sophisticated tool that can help you perform work more efficiently. As the user of this tool, you can control the way Windows NT operates, the kind of work you want to do, and how you want it done.

In this section, you'll learn more about menus and commands, as well as *dialog boxes*, a type of window that presents available options or lists selections related to a command.

Opening and Closing Menus

When you go to a restaurant, you usually read a menu to see what is offered, and then choose what to order from that menu.

Similarly, Windows NT provides a variety of menus you can use to choose and perform different tasks. The most frequently used menu in Windows NT is the Start menu. When you want to accomplish a particular task with your computer, you begin by clicking the Start button on the taskbar. This tells Windows NT to start working.

When you click the Start button, the Start menu appears and presents a list of commands from which you can choose. You can then select a command that indicates the direction you want to go to start working. You might elect to run a program, open a document, write an electronic mail message, play a game, or look for a file.

In addition to the Start menu, there are many windows and programs that have their own sets of menus and commands.

Open and close menus

You can also open the Start menu by pressing CTRL+ESC or ALT+S. You can close any open menu by pressing ESC.

1   Click the Start button.

    The Start menu opens.

2   Click an empty space on the Desktop.

    The Start menu closes.

3   On the taskbar, click My Computer.

    The My Computer window appears on top of any other open windows. Across the top of the My Computer window is a list of menu names: File, Edit, View, and Help. This list is called the *menu bar*.

4   On the menu bar on the My Computer window, click View.

    The View menu opens. Your screen should look similar to the following illustration.

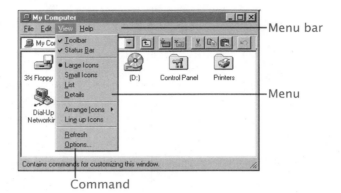

Menu bar

Menu

Command

5 On the menu bar, point to Help.

The View menu closes and the Help menu opens.

6 Click an empty space in the My Computer window.

The Help menu closes.

 TIP You can activate the menu bar in an active window by pressing ALT. The active window is the one whose title bar is colored and in which you can select menus, click toolbar buttons, or perform other actions. When you press ALT, the first menu on the menu bar is highlighted. You can use the arrow keys on the keyboard to move to the different menus, and then press ENTER to open the selected menu.

Choosing Commands

In a restaurant, once you have looked over the menu and made your decision, you tell the waiter what you have chosen, and the waiter carries out your order.

You can think of Windows NT as your waiter, taking orders based on your choices from a menu. The command you choose depends on which task you want Windows NT to perform. While the menus list all the available commands, clicking the command name actually carries it out.

A right-pointing arrow next to a menu name indicates that it opens another menu—a cascading menu.

Open menus by pointing

1 Click the Start button.

The Start menu opens.

2 Point to Programs.

The Programs menu opens to the right of the Start menu.

3 On the Programs menu, point to Accessories.

The Accessories menu opens to the right of the Programs menu.

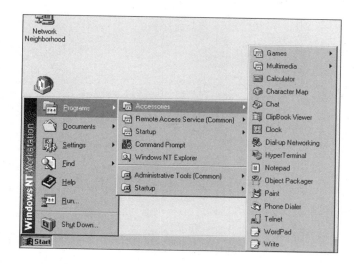

4   On the Start menu, point to Settings.

The Accessories and Programs menus close, and the Settings menu opens to the right of the Start menu.

5   Click an empty area of the Desktop.

The Start and Settings menus close.

Choose commands by clicking

Each item that does not have a right-pointing arrow after its name is a command that you can perform by clicking the command name.

1   Click the Start button.

The Start menu opens.

2   Click Shut Down.

The Shut Down dialog box opens and offers you choices about shutting down Windows NT.

3   Click the No button.

The Shut Down dialog box closes without shutting down Windows NT.

4   On the My Computer window, click File on the menu bar.

The File menu opens.

5   On the File menu, click Close.

The My Computer window closes.

6   On the Recycle Bin window, click File.

7   On the File menu, click Close.

The Recycle Bin window closes. Your Desktop should look similar to the following illustration.

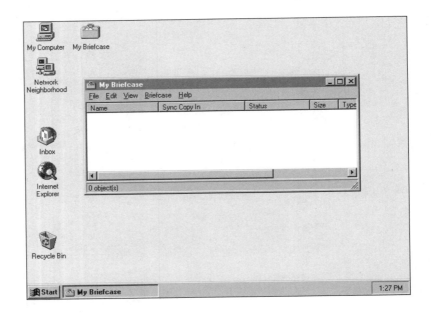

Specifying Options in Dialog Boxes

When you give your order in a restaurant, sometimes the waiter needs more information about your meal choices, such as whether you want soup or salad.

In the same way, some Windows NT commands require more information from you before they can be carried out. For example, when you choose the Run command on the Start menu, Windows NT needs more information about the location of the program you want to run. You specify this additional information through windows called *dialog boxes*. When you choose a command followed by ellipses (...), a dialog box appears.

Dialog boxes can take many different forms, but they always display choices or areas in which you select or enter the required additional information. Once you have specified the required information, the program can carry out the command you selected. The following table summarizes the most common ways to respond to the options in a dialog box.

To use this dialog box option	Do this
Check box A small square next to a word or phrase. 	Click in the square to select or clear the option. When a check mark or an "X" appears, the option is selected.

To use this dialog box option	Do this
Command button A rectangular button labeled with a command name. 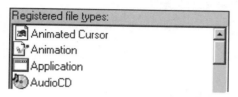	Click the button to carry out the command. This action often closes the dialog box. Many dialog boxes include three command buttons labeled OK, Cancel, and Help.
List box A box containing a list of items. A list box sometimes includes an arrow that makes the list drop downward.	Click the desired item to select it. If it is a drop-down list box, you can click the downward-pointing arrow first to display the option list.

Registered file types:
- Animated Cursor
- Animation
- Application
- AudioCD

Option button A round button next to a word or a phrase that represents one option in a set of mutually exclusive options. 	Click the button to select the option. When a black dot appears, the option is active. Only one option button in a set can be selected at one time.
Text box A rectangular box in which you can enter text (letters, numbers, or symbols) using the keyboard.	Click inside the box to display the insertion point—a blinking, vertical bar. Then, type over or edit the text. If there is a downward-pointing arrow on the right side of the box, you can click the arrow to display a list of items from which you can choose.

Specify options in a dialog box

1 Click Start.

The Start menu appears.

2 Click Run.

The Run dialog box appears.

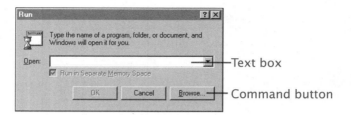

Text box

Command button

3 Click the Browse button.

The Browse dialog box appears.

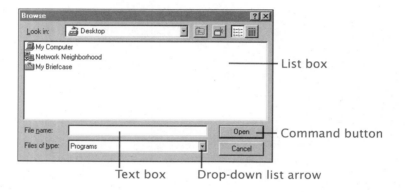

List box

Command button

Text box   Drop-down list arrow

4 Click the Cancel button.

The Browse dialog box closes, and the Run dialog box is active again.

5 If there is text in the Open text box, be sure to completely select it, and then press DELETE to clear the text.

6 Type **calc** in the Open text box, and then click the OK button.

The Calculator accessory starts, as shown in the following illustration.

Managing the Windows on Your Desktop

Just as you might have several pieces of paper or file folders lying on your desk, you can have several different windows open on your Desktop at the same time. You can manage the size, position, and visibility of these windows to quickly display and work in the window you want.

Although the window looks like a simple rectangle full of information, it is a flexible object. There are several graphic controls on every window that let you manage its position and size. The following illustration and table detail these controls.

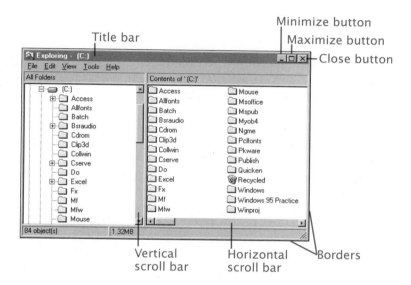

Window element	Description and function
Title bar	The bar at the top edge of every window, showing its name. By dragging this bar, you can move the window around the Desktop. When the title bar is highlighted, the window is active.
Minimize button	A button in the upper-right corner of most windows which looks like a single line. Clicking this button hides the window, but the program continues running and a button with its name remains on the taskbar. You can restore the window by clicking the taskbar button.

Window element	Description and function
Maximize button	A button in the upper-right corner of most windows (unless the window has already been maximized, which looks like a single window. Clicking this button enlarges the window to fill the entire screen.
Restore button	A button in the upper-right corner of a maximized window which looks like two overlapping windows. Clicking this button resets the window to its previous size and position.
Close button	A button in the upper-right corner of all windows, which looks like an "X." Clicking this button closes the window and removes the corresponding button from the taskbar.
Borders	The visible lines surrounding all the sides of a window which has not been maximized. Dragging a side of the border changes the height or width of the window. Dragging a corner changes the height and width of the window simultaneously.
Horizontal scroll bar	The horizontal bar that appears along the bottom of any window when the window contains information that is wider than the window's current width. The scroll bar moves the display of the window's contents horizontally, without changing the window's size or location.
Vertical scroll bar	The vertical bar that appears along the right side of any window when the window contains information that is longer than the window's current height. The scroll bar moves the display of the window's contents vertically, without changing the window's size or location.

In the following exercises, you'll use each of the window controls to manage the windows on your Desktop.

Sizing and Moving Windows

Sizing and moving windows is especially useful when you have several windows open on your Desktop and want to view a window that's obscured by another, or when you want to view two windows side by side.

Maximize and restore a window

1 Double-click the My Computer icon. If necessary, drag the Calculator title bar to move the Calculator window out of the way.

The My Computer window appears.

Maximize

2 On the upper-right corner of the My Computer window, click the Maximize button.

The My Computer window enlarges to fill the entire screen. The Maximize button changes to the Restore button.

Restore

3 Click the Restore button.

The My Computer window returns to its previous size and location. The Restore button changes to the Maximize button.

Minimize and restore a window

Minimize

1 On the upper-right corner of the My Computer window, click the Minimize button.

The My Computer window disappears, but a button with its name remains on the taskbar at the bottom of the screen.

2 Click the My Computer button on the taskbar.

The My Computer window returns to its previous size and location on the Desktop.

Resize a window

1 Position the mouse pointer on the right border of the My Computer window.

The pointer shape changes to a two-headed arrow pointing left and right.

2 Drag the border approximately one inch to the left to make the window smaller.

3 Point to the top border of the My Computer window.

The pointer shape changes to a two-headed arrow pointing upward and downward.

4 Drag the border approximately two inches downward to make it narrower.

5 Point to the lower-left corner of the My Computer window.

The pointer shape changes to a two-headed diagonal arrow.

6 Drag the border diagonally, approximately one inch upward and one inch to the right.

Your window size changes accordingly.

Move a window

1 Point to the words "My Computer" in the title bar.

2 Drag the title bar of the My Computer window until the window is positioned in the upper-left corner of the Desktop.

3 Drag the title bar of the My Computer window until the window is positioned in the lower-right corner of the Desktop.

4 Drag the My Computer window back to the center of the Desktop.

Scrolling the Contents of a Window

If a window is large enough to display its entire contents, it is surrounded only by a title bar and borders. However, when you increase the contents of the window, or decrease its size, parts of the window contents can become hidden. When this happens, a set of scroll bars appears on the right and bottom edges of the window. You can use these horizontal and vertical bars to bring hidden portions of the window contents into view.

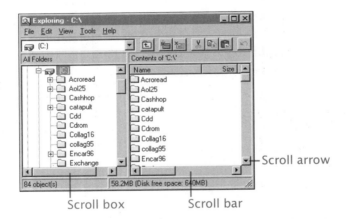

Scroll arrow

Scroll box   Scroll bar

A *scroll bar* is a band that appears along the window's right edge for vertical scrolling, or along the bottom edge for horizontal scrolling. Each scroll bar contains scroll arrows and a scroll box. When a scroll bar appears on your window, it indicates that the window contains more information than is currently visible.

The *scroll arrows* appear on either side of the scroll bar. You can use these arrow buttons to move the scroll box in either direction.

The *scroll box* is the rectangle that appears inside the scroll bar. Its relative location on the scroll bar indicates the position of the window's visible contents relative to its total contents. You can drag the scroll box to scroll the window contents faster than with the scroll arrows, though the scroll arrows give you more precision in scrolling.

Scroll a window

1 Drag the lower-right corner of the My Computer window until the window is about two inches square.

Vertical and horizontal scroll bars appear on the My Computer window. Your screen should look similar to the following illustration.

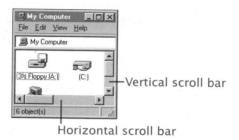

Vertical scroll bar

Horizontal scroll bar

2 On the vertical scroll bar, click the down arrow twice.

Other items in the My Computer window appear.

3 On the horizontal scroll bar, click the light gray scroll bar area to the right of the scroll box.

Other items in the My Computer window come into view.

4 Drag the horizontal scroll box to the left.

5 Drag the borders of the My Computer window until the window is close to the size it was when you first opened it.

One Step Further: Organizing Windows Using Shortcut Menus

In addition to managing individual windows on your Desktop, you can quickly organize all the screen elements by using shortcut menus.

1 Use the right mouse button to click an empty area of the taskbar.

A shortcut menu appears, displaying commands for arranging windows on your Desktop.

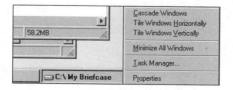

2   Click Cascade Windows.

All open windows are arranged on the Desktop in a cascading fashion, with the title bars of each window showing.

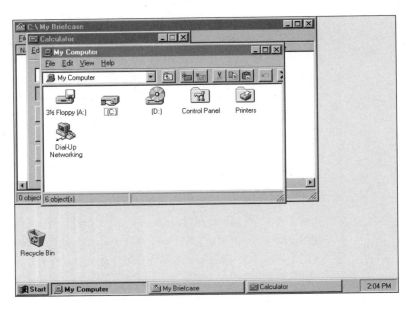

3   Use the right mouse button to click an empty area of the taskbar.

4   On the shortcut menu, click Tile Windows Horizontally.

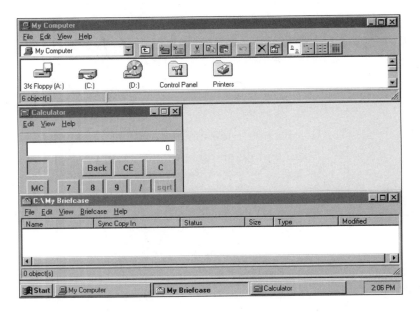

5 Use the right mouse button to click on the My Computer icon. Drag other windows to the right if necessary.

6 On the shortcut menu, click Properties.

The System Properties dialog box appears.

7 Click OK.

Finish the lesson

Close

1 Close all open windows by clicking the Close button in the upper-right corner of each window.

2 If any window is minimized, use the right mouse button to click its button on the taskbar, and then click Close.

You are now ready to start the next lesson, or you can work on your own.

3 If you are finished using Windows NT for now, on the Start menu, click Shut Down, and then click Yes.

Lesson Summary

To	Do this	Button
Click an item with the mouse	Point to the item, and press and release the mouse button.	
Double-click an item with the mouse	Point to the item, and press and release the mouse button twice in rapid succession.	
Drag an item on the Desktop	Point to the item, hold down the mouse button, slide the mouse so that the pointer moves to the new location, and then release the mouse button.	
Open a menu	Click the menu name on the menu bar.	
Close a menu without executing a command	Click an empty area on the Desktop.	
Choose a command	Click a command name on a menu.	
Maximize a window to fill the Desktop	Click the Maximize button on the window.	
Restore a maximized window to its previous size	Click the Restore button on the window.	

To	Do this	Button
Minimize a window	Click the Minimize button on the window.	![minimize button]
Restore a minimized window	Click the button labeled with the item's name on the taskbar.	
Resize a window	Drag one of the borders or corners of the window.	
Move a window	Drag the window's title bar.	
Scroll the contents of a window	Drag the scroll box.	
Close a window	Click the Close button on the window.	![close button]

For online information about	In the Help Topics dialog box, click Index, and then type
Using the mouse	**mouse**
Using menus	**menus**
Using dialog boxes	**dialog boxes, using**
Controlling the size and position of a window	**window**

Getting Around in Windows NT Workstation

In this lesson you will learn how to:

- Locate and start documents and programs.
- Activate and control documents and programs using the taskbar.
- Learn about Windows NT and look up topics using the online Help system.

Estimated time
30 min.

When starting a new job, once you feel comfortable with your immediate working area, you might take a tour of your building. You'd probably learn where the supplies are, where the coffee is, who's who, and what the best way to get things done is.

In Lesson 1, you learned how to manage the individual windows and other objects that appear on your Desktop, and how to give commands to the computer. Now, you're ready to find out how to locate and open the documents and programs located on your computer. These documents and programs are the tools you use daily to complete your work.

Starting Programs in Windows NT

When you work, you use different tools and equipment to accomplish the tasks associated with your job. When you work on a computer, you use a variety of programs to create different types of documents and to perform different kinds of work. A *program* is a detailed set of logical instructions to the computer, tell-

23

ing it to perform a specific task or a group of related tasks. For example, the job of a simple program might be to display the time on your Desktop. The job of a more complex program, such as the Microsoft Excel spreadsheet program, might be to perform calculations and draw graphs based on numeric data. Windows NT comes with a number of built-in programs, called *accessories*, that can be used for different purposes. One easy way you can locate and start many of these programs is to use the Start button on the taskbar.

Calculator program

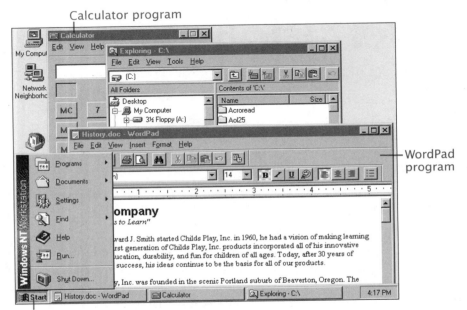

WordPad program

Start button

Start and use a program

Suppose you need to write a memo. In this exercise, you start WordPad, a simple text editing program that comes with Windows NT as an accessory.

1   If your computer isn't already on, turn it on now. If necessary, press CTRL+ALT+DELETE to log on. Type your password if you're using one, and then press ENTER. If you see the Welcome dialog box, click the Close button.

2   Click the Start button.

   The Start menu appears.

3   On the Start menu, point to Programs.

   As soon as you point to Programs, the Programs cascading menu appears.

4 On the Programs menu, point to Accessories.

The Accessories cascading menu appears.

5 On the Accessories menu, click WordPad.

WordPad opens, and the title of the WordPad window appears on the taskbar.

If your screen looks different from this illustration, refer to Appendix B, "Matching the Exercises."

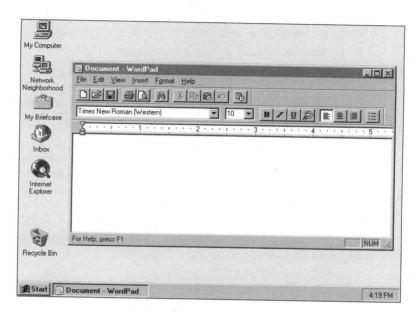

Finding Documents in Windows NT

To find a particular document on your computer, such as a letter, you need to understand how computers store information. All information on a computer is stored in *files*, individually named sets of information. When you use a program to enter a letter, for example, into the computer, you store it in a *document file* (usually just called a *document*). The documents you create might include letters, reports, presentations, tables, graphics, charts, and detailed lists.

As you work, you will probably create a lot of documents. You can keep them organized in *folders*. Folders are comparable to file folders in a filing cabinet. Each folder can hold one or more documents. Your folders are stored on the *hard disk*, which is like a huge filing cabinet inside your computer. Your folders and documents can also be stored on a *floppy disk*, like the one holding the practice files that came with this book. A floppy disk is like a small, portable filing cabinet for your computer.

You probably think of your work in terms of the end product, such as a letter, rather than in terms of what program you used to create the letter, such as Microsoft Word. In Windows NT, you can find the various documents you create, and then open them directly, without first having to find and open the program that was used to create them. You can use three different tools to locate your documents, whether they are stored in folders, disk drives, or even on other computers on your network system:

- Windows NT Explorer
- My Computer and Network Neighborhood icons
- Documents menu

Finding Documents Using Windows NT Explorer

With *Windows NT Explorer*, you can search through and get into computers, disk drives, folders, and files on your computer and network. Although you'll be learning more about Windows NT Explorer in Lesson 7, "Sharing Information with Other People On Your Network," the next exercise is a quick preview.

Open documents using *Windows NT Explorer*

In this exercise, you look for a document file, stored on your system, that outlines the history of Childs Play, Inc. You'll use Windows NT Explorer to browse through your system.

1   Click Start.

The Start menu appears.

2   On the Start menu, point to Programs.

The Programs menu appears.

3   On the Programs menu, click Windows NT Explorer.

Windows NT Explorer starts, and a button representing it and entitled "Exploring" appears on the taskbar.

4   In the left half of the window of Windows NT Explorer, titled All Folders, click (C:).

5   In the right half of the window, titled Contents Of '(C:)', find the Windows NT Practice folder and double-click it. You might need to use the scroll bar to find the folder.

The contents of the Windows NT Practice folder appear in the contents list.

6   In the contents list, find the WordPad document called History, and double-click it.

Close

Minimize

7 Click the Close button in the upper-right corner of the History document window.

The document and WordPad close.

8 In the left half of the Windows NT Explores window titled All Folders, click (C:).

9 Click the Minimize button in the upper-right corner of the Exploring window, and then in the Document-WordPad window.

> **TIP** To start a program in Windows NT Explorer, double-click the program filename. For example, to start Microsoft Excel without opening an existing workbook, locate the folder in which the Microsoft Excel program file is stored, and then double-click the program filename (in this case, Excel).

Getting Around in the Computer Community

Windows NT displays a few standard icons on your Desktop to graphically organize the files on your computer system.

These icons symbolize your computing community. The My Computer icon represents the computer on which you are actually working; you can think of it as your home base. When you open My Computer, you can view the folders and files that are stored on your own computer's disk drives. You can also see any other disk drives and computers on your network to which you have an active connection.

If My Computer is home base, then Network Neighborhood represents the outside community that provides different types of services to which you have access. When you open Network Neighborhood, you can view the folders and files that are stored on other computers on your network.

You'll learn more about the standard icons in Lessons 7 and 8. However, you can start familiarizing yourself with them in the following exercises.

View files on the available computers

Suppose you're looking for a particular file that's stored somewhere on your computer system, but you're not exactly sure where. In this exercise, you open My Computer and Network Neighborhood to see the files and folders stored there, and browse through them.

1 Double-click the My Computer icon.

The My Computer window opens, listing the icons and names of the disk drives on your computer. There are also folders for the Control Panel and Printers.

When you double-click an icon...

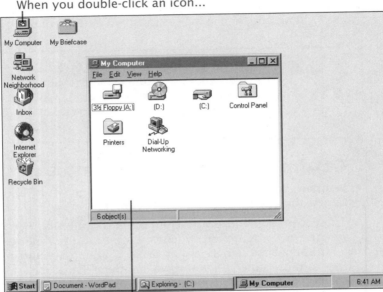

...the window for that icon opens.

2 Double-click the Network Neighborhood icon.

The Network Neighborhood window appears. You'll see a list of the various computers, disks, and public folders for your workgroup, as well as the Entire Network icon.

3 Click the Close button to close the Network Neighborhood window.

Close

Change drives and folders in My Computer

You think that the file might be on a floppy disk instead of the hard disk. In this exercise, you change disk drives to browse through the files stored on a floppy disk.

1 Be sure that the My Computer window is active.

2 Insert the Windows NT Step by Step practice disk into your floppy disk drive.

3 Double-click the appropriate floppy disk icon (A or B) in the My Computer window to switch to it.

A new window opens displaying the contents of your floppy disk. Your screen should look similar to the following illustration.

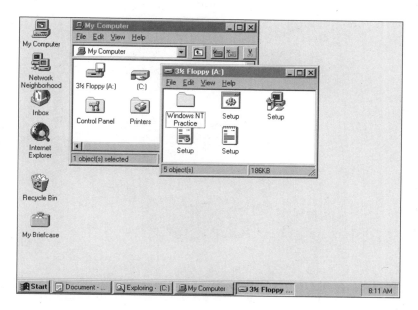

4   Double-click the Windows NT Practice folder, and then double-click the Marketing folder icon.

   A new window opens, displaying the contents of the Marketing folder.

5   Click the Close button to close the Marketing window.

6   Click the Close button to close the Windows NT Practice window and the 3 ½ inch Floppy window.

7   Remove the Windows NT Step by Step Practice disk from your floppy disk drive.

Open documents and programs in My Computer

While browsing through My Computer, you found the file you've been looking for. In this exercise, you open the logo file from a window in My Computer.

1   In the My Computer window, double-click the (C:) icon.

   The (C:) window appears, displaying the names of the files and folders stored on your hard disk.

2   Double-click the Windows NT Practice folder.

   The Windows NT Practice folder appears, displaying the names of the files and folders it contains.

3 Double-click the Logo Yellows file.

The Logo Yellows file opens in Paint, a program provided as a Windows NT accessory. Your screen should look similar to the following illustration.

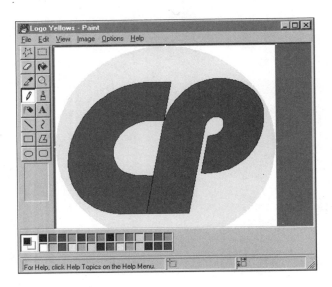

Opening Documents You Recently Used

While working on a project, you often return to the same documents in successive work sessions. Instead of having to search for these documents every time, you can use the Windows NT Documents menu to quickly access the files you most recently worked on. The Documents menu displays the last 15 documents you opened, regardless of where they are stored.

Open your recent work

You now want to open the History document you referred to earlier in this lesson to make a few changes, and then print it. In this exercise, you use the Documents menu to quickly find the file.

1 Click Start. On the Start menu, point to Documents.

The Documents menu appears.

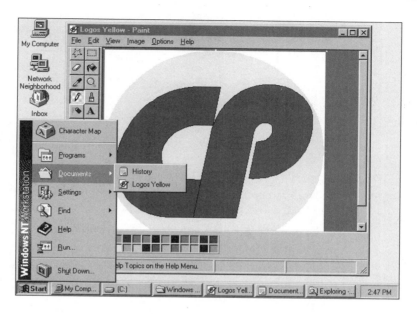

2   On the Documents menu, click History.

The History document opens in WordPad. You can now make changes and print the document.

Managing Multiple Windows

In a typical day, you might work on two or three projects at the same time. Or, you might refer to one project while working on another. With Windows NT, you can work on multiple projects at the same time, with each project running in its own window. And, with the taskbar, it's easy to find and access all your open windows.

The taskbar lists any open documents or programs, whether or not their windows are visible. You can use the taskbar to manipulate the various programs you are running. The taskbar is always visible on the bottom edge of your Desktop, unless you explicitly hide it.

As soon as you start a program or open a window of any kind, its name appears on the taskbar. If you open another window, and then want to view the first window again, you can click its name on the taskbar.

Manage multiple windows with the taskbar

You now have several documents and programs open. In this exercise, you practice using the taskbar to view what you need when you need it.

Minimize

1 Be sure that the History-WordPad window is the active window.

2 Click the Minimize button near the upper-right corner of the History window.

The History-WordPad window is reduced to a button on the taskbar and the document no longer appears anywhere on your Desktop.

3 Click the Minimize button on the Logo Yellows-Paint window.

The Logo Yellows-Paint window disappears, but its button remains on the taskbar.

4 On the taskbar, click the History-WordPad button.

The History-WordPad window becomes active, and is restored to its previous size and place on your Desktop.

5 On the taskbar, click Document-WordPad.

The blank WordPad window becomes the active window.

Close

6 On the Document-WordPad window, click the Close button.

The document closes, and the Document-WordPad button disappears from the taskbar.

7 On the taskbar, click Exploring-(C:).

Windows NT Explorer becomes the active window.

8 Quit Windows NT Explorer by clicking its Close button.

Windows NT Explorer closes. Its button is removed from the taskbar.

Hiding and Showing the Taskbar

Suppose you need to see your entire page on your screen and you don't want your taskbar using up some of that screen space. You can hide the taskbar and keep your Desktop as open and available as possible.

Hide the taskbar

Imagine that you're working on a document for which you need every square inch of space on your Desktop. In this exercise, you hide the taskbar so that you can see the entire screen.

Maximize

1 On the taskbar, click History-WordPad.

2 On the History-WordPad window, click the Maximize button.

3 Click Start. On the Start menu, point to Settings.

4 On the Settings menu, click Taskbar.

The Taskbar Properties dialog box appears.

5 Be sure that the Taskbar Options tab is active.

6 Select the Auto Hide check box, and then click OK.

Your taskbar is hidden.

View a temporarily hidden taskbar

When your taskbar is hidden, you still might need to use it from time to time. In this exercise, you bring the hidden taskbar into view temporarily.

1 Move your mouse pointer off the screen at the bottom edge of your Desktop.

The hidden taskbar reappears.

2 Click Start. On the Start menu, point to Programs, and then click Windows NT Explorer.

The taskbar remains visible until Windows NT Explorer appears. Then, the taskbar disappears.

Show a hidden taskbar

In this exercise, you restore the original settings so that your taskbar always appears.

1 Move your mouse pointer off the screen at the bottom edge of your Desktop.

The hidden taskbar reappears.

2 Click Start. On the Start menu, point to Settings.

3 On the Settings menu, click Taskbar.

The Taskbar Properties dialog box appears. Be sure that the Taskbar Options tab is active.

4 Clear the Auto Hide check box, and then click OK.

Your taskbar appears again at the bottom of your Desktop.

Getting Help with Windows NT

When you're at work and you need to find out more information about how to do a project, you might ask a co-worker or consult a reference book. When you need information about a procedure or how to use a particular feature on your computer, the online Help system is one of the most efficient ways to learn. The online Help system for Windows NT is available from the Start menu, and lets you choose the type of help you want in the Help dialog box.

For instructions on broad categories, you can look at the Contents tab. Or, you can search the Index tab for information on specific topics. The Help information is short and concise, and provides the exact information you need quickly. There are also shortcut buttons in many Help topics that you can use to switch directly to the task you want to perform.

Viewing Help Contents

The Contents tab is organized like a book's table of contents. As you choose top-level topics, or chapters, you see a list of more detailed topics from which to choose. Many of these chapters have special "Tips and Tricks" subsections that can help you work more efficiently.

Find Help on general categories

Suppose you want to learn more about using the Calculator, a program that comes with Windows NT. In this exercise, you look up information in the online Help system.

1 Click Start. On the Start menu, click Help.

The Help Topics dialog box appears. If this is the first time you've opened Help since you set up Windows NT, you might need to wait a few minutes while Windows NT sets up the Help system.

2 If necessary, click the Contents tab to make it active.

3 Double-click "Introducing Windows NT."

A set of topics appears.

4 Double-click "Using Windows Accessories."

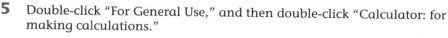

5 Double-click "For General Use," and then double-click "Calculator: for making calculations."

A Help topic window appears.

Maximize

6 Click the Maximize button on the Windows NT Help window.

The Windows NT Help window fills the entire screen.

7 Click the Close button to close the Windows NT Help window.

Finding Help on Specific Topics

You can use either the Index tab or the Find tab to locate specific Help topics. In the Index tab, you use alphabetically organized keywords to setup search criteria. You can either scroll through the list of keywords or type the keyword you want to find. One or more topic choices are then presented. With the Find tab, you can also enter a keyword. The main difference is that you get a list of all Help topics in which that keyword appears, not just the topics that begin with that word.

Find Help on specific topics using the Help index

In this exercise, you use the Help index to learn how to change the background pattern of your Desktop.

1 Click Start. On the Start menu, click Help.

The Help Topics dialog box appears.

2 Click the Index tab to make it active.

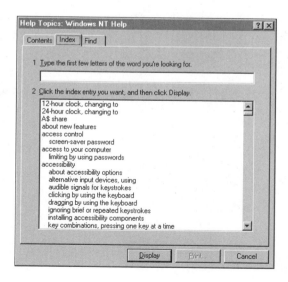

3 In the box under step 1, type **display**

A list of display-related topics appears.

4 Double-click the topic named "display, background pictures or patterns, changing."

5 Double-click the topic named "Changing the background of your desktop."

6 Read the Help topic.

7 Click the button marked with an arrow in step 1 of the Help topic.

The Display Properties dialog box appears.

8 Click the Close button on the Display Properties dialog box.

9 Click the Close button on the Windows Help window.

Jump

Close

 TIP You can easily print any Help topic by clicking the Options button in the upper-left corner of any Help topic window, and then clicking Print Topic.

Find Help on specific topics using the Find tab

In this exercise, you use the Find tab to learn how to change your printer's settings.

1 Click Start. On the Start menu, click Help.

The Help Topics dialog box appears.

2 Click the Find tab to make it active.

3 If this is the first time that you have used this tab, a wizard will appear. Be sure to select the recommended option button, and then click Next. Click Finish to exit the wizard.

The Find tab appears.

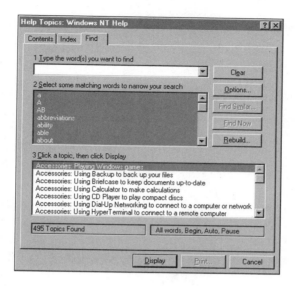

4 In the box under step 1, type **print**

All topics that have to do with printing are displayed in the box at the bottom of the dialog box.

5 In the box under step 3, click the "Changing printer settings" topic, and then click Display.

A Help window containing the topic titled "To change printer settings" appears.

6 Read the Help topic using the scroll bar to display the rest of the topic if necessary.

7 Click the Close button on the Windows NT Help window.

Get Help on choices in a dialog box

Almost every dialog box includes a question mark button in the upper-right corner. When you click this button, and then click any dialog box control, a Help window appears that explains what the control is and how to use it. In this exercise, you get help on specific elements in a dialog box by using context-sensitive Help.

1 Click Start. On the Start menu, click Run.

The Run dialog box appears.

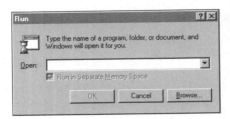

Help

2   In the Run dialog box, click the Help button in the upper-right corner.

The mouse pointer changes to an arrow with a question mark.

3   Click the Open box.

A pop-up window appears, providing information on how to use the Open box.

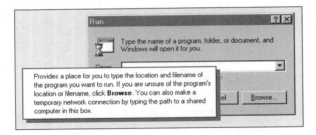

4   Click anywhere in the Run dialog box, or press ESC.

5   Click the Help button again, and then click Browse.

Help displays information about the Browse button.

6   Click Browse.

The Browse dialog box appears.

7   Click the Help button, and then click the Files Of Type box.

A pop-up window appears containing information about the Files Of Type box.

8   Click Cancel.

9   In the Run dialog box, click Cancel.

 TIP   You can change the way the Help topics appear on your screen by clicking the Options button in the menu bar of any Help topic window, and then pointing to Font to change the font size.

One Step Further: Move and Change the Size of the Taskbar

You can move the taskbar to any of the four sides of your Desktop. You can also make the taskbar wider.

1   Click an empty space on the taskbar, and then drag it to the right edge of your Desktop.

The taskbar is positioned along the right side of your screen.

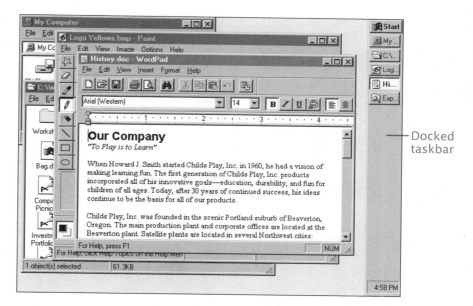

Docked taskbar

2   Drag the taskbar to the top of your Desktop.

The taskbar is positioned at the top of your screen.

3   Drag the taskbar back to the bottom of your Desktop.

The taskbar returns to its original position.

4   Move the mouse pointer to the inside edge of the taskbar so that its shape changes to a two-headed arrow.

5   Drag the edge of the taskbar upward to widen it.

6   Drag the edge of the taskbar downward to return it to its original size.

Finish the lesson

Close

1 Close all the open windows by clicking the Close button in the upper-right corner of each window.

2 If any window is minimized, use the right mouse button to click the window's taskbar button, and then click Close.

You are now ready to start the next lesson, or you can work on your own.

3 If you are finished using Windows NT for now, on the Start menu, click Shut Down, make sure the Shut Down The Computer option is selected, and then click Yes.

Lesson Summary

To	Do this	Button
Start a program	Click Start, point to Programs, and then click the program name.	
Start Windows NT Explorer	Click Start, point to Programs, and then click Windows NT Explorer.	
Open a document	In Windows NT Explorer, find the document, and then double-click its name.	
Open a recently used document	Click Start, point to Documents, and then click the document name.	
View and open the contents of disks, folders, or files on your computer	Double-click the My Computer icon, and then double-click the disks, folders, or file icons you want.	
View and open the contents of computers, disks, or public folders on the network	Double-click the Network Neighborhood icon, and then double-click the disks, folders, or file icons you want.	
Manage multiple windows with the taskbar	Click the Minimize button of any open window to reduce it to a taskbar button. Click any taskbar button to restore or activate the window it represents.	▬
Hide the taskbar	Click Start, point to Settings, and then click Taskbar. Click the Taskbar Options tab, select the Auto Hide check box, and then click OK.	

To	Do this
Temporarily view a hidden taskbar	Move the mouse pointer close to the edge of the Desktop where the taskbar was last positioned. If you're not sure where the taskbar was positioned, move the mouse pointer to all four edges of the Desktop until the taskbar appears.
Show a hidden taskbar	Click Start, point to Settings, and then click Taskbar. Click the Taskbar Options tab, clear the Auto Hide check box, and then choose OK.
Find Help on a general topic	Click Start, click Help, click the Contents tab, and then double-click the topic you want.
Find Help on a specific topic	Click Start, click Help, click the Index or Find tab, type a keyword, and then click Display.
Find Help on a dialog box	Click the Help button on the dialog box, and then click the dialog box control for which you want help.

For online information about	In the Help Topics dialog box, click Index, and then type
Opening programs using the Start button	**opening, programs**
Opening documents using the Start button	**opening, files**
Using the My Computer icon	**My Computer**
Using the Network Neighborhood icon	**Network Neighborhood**
Managing documents and programs using the taskbar	**taskbar**
Finding online Help	**Help**

Customizing Your Desktop for the Way You Work

In this lesson you will learn how to:

Estimated time
40 min.

- Quickly access frequently used programs by adding commands to your Start and Programs menus.
- Create shortcuts to frequently used files, and display these shortcuts as Desktop icons.
- Configure your mouse to fit the way you work.
- Customize your Windows NT display to suit your preferences.

People often tailor their work areas with an eye toward comfort and efficiency. Sometimes this involves arranging furniture, adding plants, or hanging artwork on the walls. It's also convenient to have within reach the tools, equipment, and supplies you use most often.

In Microsoft Windows NT, you can change various aspects of your work environment. You can customize your menus to quickly start the programs you use the most. You can create shortcuts to documents you frequently open. You can also individualize your display and your mouse. In this lesson, you'll find out how you can create an environment that reflects your individual style and work habits.

Customizing Menus So You Can Easily Access Commands

If you use your telephone, fax machine, stapler, or tape dispenser on a regular basis, you probably have them on or near your desk for easy and convenient access. Similarly in Windows NT, shortcuts to programs are automatically added to the Start and Programs menus during the installation process so that you can access them quickly. You can also customize your menus as well as organize your Start menu to reflect the way you work and speed up your access to the programs you use most often.

You can also remove items that you rarely use from your Start and Programs menus.

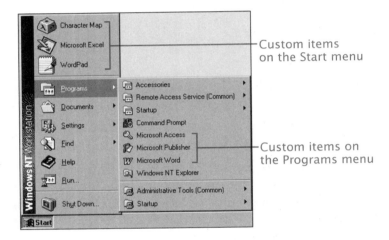

Custom items on the Start menu

Custom items on the Programs menu

Adding Commands to Your Start Menu

Adding a command to your Start menu allows you to quickly access and open any program you have set up on your computer.

Add commands to your Start menu

Character Map is a Windows NT accessory used mainly for inserting special characters and symbols into your documents. Suppose you are referring to Character Map daily and want it to be more easily accessible. In this exercise, you add Character Map to your Start menu.

1   If your computer isn't already on, turn it on now. If necessary, press CTRL+ALT+DELETE to log on. Type your password if you're using one, and then press ENTER. If you see the Welcome dialog box, click the Close button.

2 Click Start. On the Start menu, point to Settings.

3 On the Settings menu, click Taskbar, and then click the Start Menu Programs tab.

4 Under Customize Start Menu, click Add.

The Create Shortcut dialog box appears.

You can also click the Browse button to locate the command filename.

5 In the Command Line text box, type **charmap**, and then click Next. You can follow these steps to add any additional programs to the Start menu by substituting the appropriate name in the Command Line box. If you don't know the exact name of the program you want to add, see "Finding Files" in Lesson 8.

The Select Program Folder dialog box appears.

6 Click the Start Menu folder, and then click Next.

7 Type **Character Map**, and then click Finish.

8 Click OK, and then click the Start button.

The Character Map command, along with its associated icon, appears at the top of the Start menu.

Items you add to the Start menu appear in alphabetical order above the default Start menu items.

9 On the Start menu, click Character Map.

Adding Commands to Your Programs Menu

When you first start using Windows NT, the Programs menu includes a few important programs, such as Windows NT Explorer and WordPad as well as programs that were previously on your computer, if you are upgrading. You can customize the Programs menu to include the startup commands of all your installed programs, or of the programs you use most frequently. Adding program commands to the Programs menu is similar to adding commands to the Start menu. The result is similar as well—the command appears on the Programs menu rather than on the Start menu. Where you add the command—on the Programs menu or the Start menu—is simply a matter of preference.

You can also remove program commands from the Programs menu. You might, for example, want to remove commands for programs you no longer use. When you remove a command from the menu, the program itself is not deleted; it is still available. Its command is just not available from the Programs menu. You can remove any Programs menu command you want, even if you didn't add it in the first place.

The program commands you will most likely add to your Programs menu will be for additional programs, beyond those that came with Windows NT—for example, Microsoft PowerPoint or Microsoft Publisher. In the following exercises, however, you'll practice with two Windows NT accessories.

 NOTE Unlike the Start menu or Programs menu, your Documents menu cannot be customized. Whenever you open a document, a shortcut to the document is automatically added to the Documents menu. The Documents menu lists shortcuts to the last 15 documents you have opened.

Add program commands to your Programs menu

In order to speed up your work, you add frequently used programs to the Programs menu. In this exercise, you add Paint to the Programs menu.

1   Use the right mouse button to click an empty area of the taskbar.

    A shortcut menu appears.

2   On the shortcut menu, click Properties.

    The Taskbar Properties dialog box appears.

3   Click the Start Menu Programs tab, and then click Add.

4   In the Command Line text box, type **mspaint**, and then click Next.

    You can follow these steps to add any additional programs to the Start menu by substituting the appropriate name in the Command Line box. If you don't know the exact name of the program you want to add, see "Finding Files" in Lesson 8.

You can also click the Browse button to locate the command filename.

5   Click the Programs folder, and then click Next.

6   Type **Paint**, click Finish, and then click OK.

7   Click Start. On the Start menu, point to Programs.

    The Paint command appears on the Programs menu.

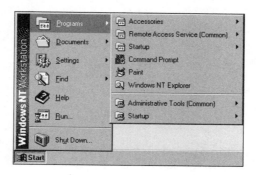

8   On the Programs menu, click Paint.

Paint starts.

Close

9   Click the Close button.

The Paint window and program close.

Remove program commands from your Programs menu

As your work progresses, you don't need to use Paint as frequently as before. In this exercise, you remove the Paint command from the Programs menu.

1   Use the right mouse button to click an empty area of the taskbar.

A shortcut menu appears.

2   Click Properties.

The Taskbar Properties dialog box appears.

3   Click the Start Menu Programs tab, and then click Remove.

4   In the Remove Shortcuts/Folders window, click Paint, and then click Remove.

5   In the Confirm File Delete dialog box, click Yes.

Paint is deleted from the Programs menu.

6   Click Close, and then click OK in the Taskbar Properties dialog box.

7   Click Start. On the Start menu, point to Programs.

Paint no longer appears as a command on the Programs menu.

8   Click an empty area on the Desktop to close the menus.

TIP You can remove any command you want (except Startup) from the Programs menu, even if it is a command that was on the Start menu when you first started using Windows NT. If you change your mind, you can always add it back again.

Using Shortcuts To Speed Up Your Work

As part of the standard setup, the My Computer, Network Neighborhood, Inbox, Internet Explorer, and Recycle Bin icons always appear on your Desktop.

While this setup is clean and sparce, you might find it useful to add *shortcuts*, icons that graphically represent programs, folders, or documents that you use frequently and which are identified by a little arrow in their lower-left corner. For example, if you use a spreadsheet program every day, or you often access a certain public folder on the network, you can create a shortcut for these programs or folders to directly access them.

Default icon

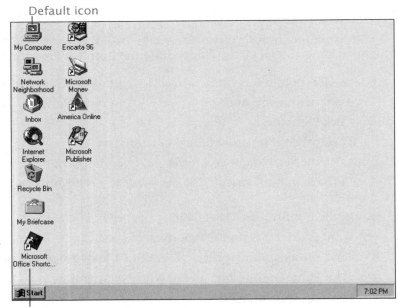

Custom shortcut icons

Creating New Shortcuts

A shortcut functions as a pointer to the actual item it represents, wherever it might be stored on your hard disk. When you double-click the icon to open the shortcut, you're opening the actual item to which the shortcut is pointing. Shortcuts are very convenient and save the time that you would have spent browsing through disk drives and perhaps several folders to find the file you needed.

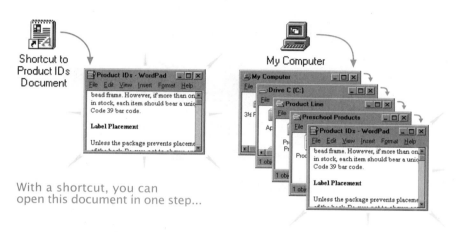

With a shortcut, you can open this document in one step...

...instead of five steps.

Create shortcut to programs

In this exercise, you use the Find command to locate the WordPad program file, and then create a shortcut to it on the Desktop.

1   Click Start. Point to Find, and then click Files Or Folders.

    The Find dialog box appears. Be sure that the Name & Location tab is active.

2   In the Named box, type **wordpad**

3   Click the Find Now button.

    A list appears, showing all files containing the term "wordpad" in their names.

4   Use the right mouse button to drag the Wordpad application file to the Desktop.

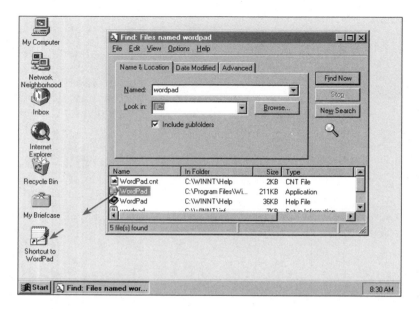

5 On the shortcut menu, click Create Shortcut(s) Here.

The Shortcut To Wordpad.exe icon appears on your Desktop. You might need to drag the Find dialog box out of the way to see the WordPad shortcut.

6 Close the Find dialog box.

Create shortcuts to folders and documents

In this exercise, you create shortcuts to two items that you use often: the Marketing folder and a logo document file.

1 Click Start. Point to Programs, and then click Windows NT Explorer.

The Exploring window appears.

2 In the Exploring window, double-click the hard drive (C:).

3 Double-click the Windows NT Practice folder.

The Windows NT Practice folder opens.

4 Use the right mouse button to drag the Marketing folder to the Desktop.

5 On the shortcut menu, click Create Shortcut(s) Here.

The Marketing folder shortcut appears on your Desktop.

6 In the Windows NT Practice folder window, use the right mouse button to drag the Logo Multicolored file to the Desktop.

7 On the shortcut menu, click Create Shortcut(s) Here.

The Logo Multicolored shortcut appears on your Desktop.

Rename shortcuts

In this exercise, you close the open windows, and then rename the three
shortcut icons so that they are more descriptive and intuitive.

1   Close all the open windows.

    Your screen should look similar to the following illustration.

2   Use the right mouse button to click the Shortcut To Wordpad icon.

3   On the shortcut menu, click Rename.

    The name "Shortcut To Wordpad" is highlighted, and a blinking inser-
    tion point appears.

4   Type **WordPad**, and then press ENTER.

    The WordPad shortcut is renamed.

5   Use the right mouse button to click the Shortcut To Marketing folder
    icon, and then, on the shortcut menu, click Rename.

6   Type **Childs Play Marketing**, and then press ENTER.

7   Use the right mouse button to click the Logo Multicolored document
    icon, and then, on the shortcut menu, click Rename.

8 Type **Color Logo**, and then press ENTER.

Your screen should look similar to the following illustration.

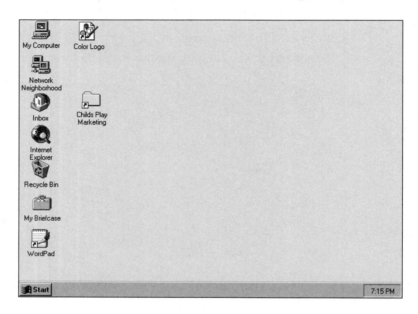

Use shortcuts

In this exercise, you use the shortcuts you created to start WordPad, open the Marketing folder, and then open the Color Logo file.

1 Double-click the WordPad shortcut.

WordPad starts, as if you had started it from the Accessories menu.

2 Double-click the Childs Play Marketing folder shortcut.

The Childs Play Marketing folder opens, displaying its contents.

3 Double-click the Color Logo shortcut.

The Color Logo graphic opens in Paint.

Maximize

4 Click the Maximize button on the Paint window to display the entire logo.

5 Close all open windows.

Managing Your Shortcuts

You can make your Desktop as spare or as full as you like. When you add more icons to your Desktop, there are additional tools available to help you manage, arrange, and work with the icons.

If you decide you no longer need a shortcut, you can remove the icon from your Desktop without deleting the object to which the shortcut is pointing.

Arrange your icons on the Desktop

You now have several icons on your Desktop. In this exercise, you arrange the icons in an orderly scheme.

1   Use the right mouse button to click an empty area of the Desktop.

   A shortcut menu appears.

2   Point to Arrange Icons, and then click By Name.

   Your shortcut icons are arranged in alphabetical order on your Desktop, after the default icons.

3   Use the right mouse button to click the Desktop again, point to Arrange Icons, and then click By Date.

   Your icons are arranged based on their creation date and time, from newest to oldest.

Drag shortcuts onto your Start menu

You might want to make WordPad and the Childs Play Marketing folder available on your Start menu. In this exercise, you add shortcuts to these items to the Start menu.

1   Drag the WordPad icon on top of the Start button.

2   Click the Start button.

   You'll see that the WordPad command is added to the Start menu.

3   Close the Start menu by clicking on an empty area of the Desktop, or by pressing ESC.

4   Drag the Childs Play Marketing folder icon on top of the Start button.

5   Click the Start button again.

   The Childs Play Marketing folder is now added as a command to the Start menu.

6   From the Start menu, click Childs Play Marketing.

   The Childs Play Marketing folder opens.

7   Close the Childs Play Marketing folder.

Remove shortcuts from your Desktop

Now that you have completed the project you were working on, you no longer need the shortcuts to WordPad, the Child Plays Marketing folder and the Color Logo graphic on your Desktop. In this exercise, you delete these shortcuts using three different methods.

1   Drag the WordPad shortcut to the Recycle Bin icon.

The WordPad shortcut is removed from the Desktop and placed in the Recycle Bin.

2   Use the right mouse button to click the Childs Play Marketing folder shortcut, and then, on the shortcut menu, click Delete.

3   In the Confirm File Delete dialog box, click Yes.

The Childs Play Marketing folder shortcut is removed from the Desktop.

4   Click the Color Logo shortcut, and then press DELETE.

5   In the Confirm File Delete dialog box, click Yes.

The Color Logo shortcut is removed from the Desktop.

 TIP   If you change your mind and want one of the deleted shortcuts back, you can double-click the Recycle Bin icon to open it, and then drag the shortcut onto the Desktop again. Items in the Recycle Bin stay there until you explicitly empty the Recycle Bin.

Reset your Start menu

In this exercise, you remove Character Map and your other shortcuts from your Start menu to return it to the original setup.

1   Use the right mouse button to click an empty area of the taskbar.

2   On the shortcut menu, click Properties.

The Taskbar Properties dialog box appears.

3   Click the Start Menu Programs tab, and then click Remove.

4   In the Remove Shortcuts/Folders dialog box, click Character Map, and then click Remove.

5   In the Confirm File Delete dialog box, click Yes.

6   Repeat steps 4 and 5 to delete the shortcuts to WordPad and the Childs Play Marketing folder.

7   Click Close, and then click OK.

8   Click Start.

The three shortcuts that you added to the Start menu in this lesson are no longer listed as commands on the Start menu.

9   Press ESC to close the Start menu.

NOTE In the Start menu, you can only remove the commands that you have added. You cannot remove the default Start commands.

Customizing Your Mouse Pointer So It Looks and Responds the Way You Want

You can customize how your mouse pointer looks and feels to fit the way you work.

Changing How Your Mouse Responds to Your Hand

The way your mouse and pointer respond to your hand and finger actions can determine the efficiency with which you can control the graphical elements in Windows NT. If you are not completely comfortable with the default settings for your mouse, you can change various them using the Control Panel. If you are left-handed, you can switch the left and right button configuration. You can increase or decrease the speed, or sensitivity, with which the pointer responds to mouse movements. You can also adjust how fast or slow your double-click action is.

Change your mouse pointer speed

If your mouse pointer seems to move slowly in relation to moving the mouse itself, you will want to increase the speed of the pointer to make it more responsive to your hand movements. In this exercise, you use the Mouse Properties dialog box to increase the mouse pointer speed.

Mouse

1 Click the Start button, point to Settings, and then click Control Panel.

2 Double-click the Mouse icon, and then click the Motion tab.

3 Drag the Pointer Speed slider a little to the right, to make it a little faster, and then click Apply.

As you move your mouse around the screen, you will notice a difference in the mouse pointer response. Make any further adjustments you want.

4 Click OK.

Change your mouse button setup

If you're left-handed, you will probably want to change the primary button to the right button, and change the secondary button to the left button. In this exercise, you change your mouse button setup.

NOTE   If you like your mouse button configuration the way it is, you can skip this exercise, or you can experiment with this exercise, and then return the mouse to its original setup afterward.

1   In the Control Panel window, double-click the Mouse icon.

2   In the Mouse Properties dialog box, click the Buttons tab.

3   Click the Left-Handed option button.

4   Click Apply.

The mouse is reconfigured to a left-handed setup. The right mouse button is now the primary button.

5   Use the right mouse button to click the Close button on the Control Panel window.

6   Unless you prefer a left-handed button configuration, revert the configuration back to the original setting.

Changing the Shape of Your Mouse Pointer

You can change the mouse pointer shape for fun, as another way to customize your Desktop. Windows NT comes with a number of animation files you can use in place of the default pointer shapes.

Change the shape of your mouse pointer

1   In the Control Panel window, double-click the Mouse icon.

2   In the Mouse Properties dialog box, click the Pointers tab.

3   In the Scheme list box, click Dinosaur.

4   Click the Apply button.

The pointer changes color to indicate the new Dinosaur mouse pointer scheme.

5   Sample the other mouse pointer schemes, and choose and apply the one that you want to use.

6   Click OK to close the Mouse Properties dialog box.

Customizing Your Display So It Looks the Way You Want

From the Windows NT Control Panel, you can design your display like you decorate your office. You can choose color schemes for different window elements, such as the menu bar, the title bar, and selected text as well as choose a particular pattern for your Desktop background.

You can also select from a variety of *screen saver* patterns, which Windows NT displays when your computer and monitor are turned on, but you aren't actively working. You define the number of minutes that need to elapse before the screen saver gets activated. You can also assign a password to your screen saver so that no one else can see what's on your monitor or use your computer when you're away from your desk.

Customize your display colors

In this exercise, you select a color scheme for your window elements.

Display

1   With the Control Panel window open, double-click the Display icon.
2   Click the Appearance tab.
3   In the Scheme box, click Plum (high color).

   The colors in the sample display change to the Plum color scheme.
4   In the Scheme list box, click Teal (VGA).

   The colors in the sample display change to the Teal color scheme.
5   Click the Apply button.

   Your Desktop colors change to the Teal color scheme.
6   Sample, and then select the color scheme you want and apply it.
7   Click OK to close the Display Properties dialog box.

TIP   If you want to change the color of an individual Desktop element, click its name in the Item list box, and then select the color you want from the Color list box. You can also change Desktop element fonts, where applicable. You can even create and save entirely new color schemes.

Select your background

In this exercise, you set the background pattern and the wallpaper for your Desktop. In general, *wallpaper* is one picture or image that you can display on your Desktop. Wallpaper may or may not cover your entire Desktop. In contrast, a *pattern* is displayed on your Desktop, but consists of a repeated design that covers the entire background.

1   With the Control Panel window still open, double-click the Display icon.
2   In the Display Properties dialog box, click the Background tab.

57

3 In the Wallpaper box, click Argyle.

The sample shows the Argyle graphic centered in the display.

4 Click the Tile option button.

The sample shows the Argyle graphic tiled across the display.

5 Click Apply.

The Argyle graphic is tiled across your Desktop.

6 In the Pattern list box, click Spinner.

7 Sample, and then choose and apply the one that you want to use.

8 Click OK to close the Display Properties dialog box.

Choose a screen saver

A *screen saver* is a continually moving pattern that Windows NT displays when you are not actively working for a number of minutes. In this exercise, you view the screen savers that come with Windows NT, and then choose and apply the one you like. You also change the screen saver wait time, which defines the number of minutes that needs to elapse before the screen saver gets displayed.

1 With the Control Panel window still open, double-click the Display icon, and then click the Screen Saver tab.

2 In the Screen Saver box, select Beziers.

The sample display shows what the Beziers screen saver looks like.

3 In the Screen Saver box, select 3D FlowerBox (OpenGL).

The sample changes to the new screen saver.

4 Click the Preview button.

The screen saver appears on your entire screen.

5 Move your mouse or press any key to stop the screen saver preview.

6 Click the Settings button.

The 3D FlowerBox Setup dialog box appears.

7 In the Shape list box, click Spring, and then click OK.

The sample offers a preview of the screen saver's new shape.

8 Sample the other screen savers, explore their settings, and then select the screen saver you want to use.

9 In the Wait box, type the number of minutes that the computer should be inactive before the screen saver starts, and then click Apply.

10 Close the Display Properties window and the Control Panel window.

NOTE Your screen saver will start whenever your computer is idle for the number of minutes you specified in the Wait box. The moving image of the screen saver temporarily takes over your screen and obscures your previous work. When you want to use your computer again, press any key on the keyboard, or move the mouse. Your screen is restored and looks exactly as you left it.

One Step Further: Starting Programs Automatically Whenever You Launch Windows NT

If you want a certain program to start as soon as Windows NT starts, you can add a shortcut to the program to your StartUp folder.

Find the file you want to use for a new StartUp shortcut

Suppose you have several invoices or other information you need to add up, and you want to have the Calculator automatically start each day when you start your computer. In this exercise, you browse through your files to find the Calculator program file, and then add it to your StartUp folder so that the Calculator starts automatically each time you start Windows NT.

1   Click Start. On the Start menu, point to Settings, and then click Taskbar.

   The Taskbar Properties dialog box appears.

2   Click the Start Menu Programs tab.

3   Click Add.

   The Create Shortcut dialog box appears.

4   Click Browse.

   The Browse dialog box appears.

5   Be sure that your hard disk name (C:) appears in the Look In box, and then double-click the Winnt folder.

   The contents of the Winnt folder appear.

6   Double-click the System32 folder.

7   Scroll through the list until you find the Calculator program file, and then double-click it.

   The Create Shortcut dialog box appears again, with the Calculator program file in the Command Line box.

8   Click Next.

   The Select Program Folder dialog box appears.

Add the shortcut to your Start folder

Now that you have located the Calculator program, you can add it to your StartUp folder.

1   In the Select Program Folder dialog box, click the Start folder, and then click Next.

2   In the next window, type **Calculator** in the Name box, and then click Finish.

    The Taskbar Properties dialog box appears.

3   Click OK.

Restart Windows NT so that the shortcut automatically starts

In this exercise, you restart your computer and verify that the Calculator starts automatically when Windows NT starts.

1   Click Start. On the Start menu, click Shut Down.

2   In the Shut Down Windows dialog box, click the Restart The Computer option button, and then click Yes.

3   If necessary, press CTRL+ALT+DELETE to log on. Type your password if you're using one, and then press ENTER. If you see the Welcome dialog box, click the Close button.

    Windows NT restarts with the Calculator running.

4   Add some numbers, if you want.

5   When you have finished, close the Calculator.

Close

Remove the shortcut from your Startup folder

In this exercise, you remove the Calculator from your Startup folder so that it no longer starts automatically when Windows NT starts.

1   Click Start. On the Start menu, point to Settings, and then click Taskbar.

2   In the Taskbar Properties dialog box, click the Start Menu Programs tab.

3   On the Start Menu Programs tab, click Remove.

4   In the Remove Shortcuts/Folder dialog box, double-click the StartUp folder.

5   Under the StartUp folder, click the Calculator shortcut, and then click Remove.

6   In the Confirm File Delete dialog box, click Yes.

7   Click Close, and then click OK.

    The Calculator shortcut is removed from the Start folder.

Finish the lesson

1 Close all the open windows.

2 If any window is minimized, use the right mouse button to click the window's taskbar button, and then, on the shortcut menu, click Close.

You are now ready to start the next lesson, or you can work on your own.

3 If you have finished using Windows NT for now, on the Start menu, click Shut Down, and then click Yes.

Lesson Summary

To	Do this
Open the Taskbar Properties dialog box	Use the right mouse button to click an empty area on the taskbar, and then click Properties.
Add a command to the Start menu or Programs menu	Open the Taskbar Properties dialog box. On the Start Menu Programs tab, click Add. Type the name of the program in the Command Line text box, and then click Next. Click the Start Menu or Programs folder, and then click Next. Type a name for the shortcut command, and then click Finish. Click OK.
Remove a command from the Start menu or Programs menu	Open the Taskbar Properties dialog box. On the Start Menu Programs tab, click Remove. Click the item to remove, and then click Remove. Click Close, and then click OK.
Add a shortcut icon to the Desktop	Locate the item, and then use the right mouse button to drag the item to the Desktop. Click Create Shortcut(s) Here.
Rename a shortcut	Use the right mouse button to click the shortcut icon. On the shortcut menu, click Rename. Type the new name, and then press ENTER.
Add a shortcut to the Start menu	Drag the shortcut icon to the Start button.

To	Do this
Remove a shortcut from the Desktop	Drag the shortcut icon to the Recycle Bin.
Open Control Panel	Click Start, point to Settings, and then click Control Panel.
Customize your mouse	In the Control Panel window, double-click the Mouse icon. In the Mouse Properties dialog box, click the appropriate tab, and then select the settings you want.
Customize your display, including the background, screen saver, and colors	Use the right mouse button to click the Desktop, and then click Properties. In the Display Properties dialog box, click the appropriate tab, and then select the settings you want.

For online information about	In the Help Topics dialog box, click Index, and then type
Customizing your Start menu	**customizing, Start menu**
Creating and using shortcuts	**shortcuts**
Customizing your Windows NT setup using the Control Panel	**Control Panel**

Review & Practice

You will review and practice how to:

Estimated time
25 min.

- Locate files, start programs, and open documents.
- Manage open items with the taskbar.
- Look up information in the online Help system.
- Add and remove commands on the Start and Programs menus.
- Create shortcuts on your Desktop.

Before you go on to Part 2, you can practice the navigation and customization skills you learned in Part 1 by working through the steps in this Review & Practice section.

Scenario

You're a new employee at Childs Play, Inc., and have just received a new computer, complete with Microsoft Windows NT. Having started to learn how to use your computer, you now want to practice your new-found skills and explore how to get around in Windows NT. You also want to customize Windows NT to fit the way you like to work.

Step 1: Start Programs and Open Documents

In this step, you locate the files, start the programs, and open the documents with which you want to work.

Start programs from your Start menu

➤ With Windows NT running, use the Start button to start WordPad, Paint, and Windows NT Explorer.

Open documents

1 Use Windows NT Explorer to open the History document, which is located in your Windows NT Practice folder.

2 Open My Computer, and browse through the appropriate disks and folders to find and open the Logo Yellows document.

For more information on	See
Starting programs in Windows NT	Lesson 2
Finding documents in Windows NT	Lesson 2

Step 2: Manage Open Items with the Taskbar

In a typical work session, you have several programs running at the same time. In this step, you minimize some windows and maximize others to organize your Desktop, but keep your programs and documents open so that you can get to them quickly.

Arrange items on your Desktop

1 Move the taskbar to the top edge of your Desktop.

2 Make the Windows NT Explorer window the active window. (Hint: On the taskbar, click Exploring-Windows NT Practice.)

3 Minimize the Windows NT Explorer window.

4 Make the window containing the History document the active window.

5 Minimize the History document window.

6 Minimize the Logo Yellows document window.

7 Minimize all other windows on the Desktop.

8 Restore the Logo Yellows document window.

Provide more working space

1 Minimize the Logo Yellows document window.

2 Hide the taskbar to give yourself more working room. (Hint: Use the right mouse button to click an empty area of the taskbar, and then click Properties.)

Restore your Desktop arrangement

1 Permanently show the taskbar.

2 Move the taskbar back to its original location, at the bottom of your Desktop.

3 Close any items that are minimized on the taskbar without opening them first. (Hint: Use the right mouse button to click the item name on the taskbar.)

For more information on	See
Managing the windows on your Desktop	Lesson 1
Managing multiple windows	Lesson 2

Step 3:   *Look Up Information in Online Help*

Because you're new to Windows NT, you rely on the online Help system to answer questions that arise as you work. In this step, you use the online Help system to search and obtain information on how to customize your taskbar, as well as learn more about changing your screen saver and managing your open windows.

Find help for a general category

1 Start the online Help system.

2 On the Contents tab, expand the topic "Tips and Tricks."

3 Expand the "For Setting Up the Desktop Efficiently" topic.

4 Open and read the "Customizing the taskbar" topic.

5 Return to the Help Topics dialog box.

Find help for a specific topic

1 On the Index tab search for "display."

2 Display and read the "Display, protecting by using a screen saver" topic.

3 Search for "window."

4 Display and read the "Display, tiling windows" topic.

5 Close Windows NT Help.

For more information on	See
Getting Help with Windows NT	Lesson 2

Step 4: Customize Your Menus

As you continue to use Windows NT, you identify which programs and utilities you tend to use most often. In this step, you add Character Map to the Start menu and Calculator to the Programs menu to help make your work more efficient.

1 Add Character Map to your Start menu. (Hint: Use the right mouse button to click the taskbar, and then click Properties.)

2 Use the Start menu to start Character Map.

3 Add Calculator to your Programs menu. (Hint: Use the Browse button to find the program.)

4 Use the Programs menu to start Calculator.

5 Close Character Map and Calculator.

For more information on	See
Customizing your menus	Lesson 3

Step 5: Create Shortcut Icons on Your Desktop

There is a program, a folder, and a document that you use nearly every day. In this step, you create shortcuts to these items so that you don't lose any time browsing through the system to locate them.

Add shortcuts to your Desktop

1 Find where the Calculator accessory is stored on your computer system. (Hint: On the Start menu, point to Find, and then click Files Or Folders. The file is called Calc.)

2 Create a shortcut to Calculator on your Desktop. (Hint: Use the right mouse button to drag.)

3 Rename this shortcut Calculator.

4 Use Windows NT Explorer to find the Letters folder in your Windows NT Practice folder.

5 Create a shortcut to the Letters folder on your Desktop.

6 Rename this shortcut Letters & Memos.

7 Open My Computer and locate the Toys Logo Color file in the Windows NT Practice folder on your hard disk.

8 Create a shortcut to the Toys Logo file on your Desktop.

9 Rename this shortcut Logo.

Use your shortcuts

1 Close any open windows on your Desktop.

2   Double-click the Calculator shortcut to start it.

3   Double-click the Letters & Memos folder shortcut to open it.

4   Double-click the Logo file shortcut to open it.

5   Close all open windows.

For more information on	See
Creating and using shortcuts	Lesson 3

Step 6: *Restore Your Windows NT Default Settings*

In this step, you will reverse the changes you've made in this Review & Practice section so that your Windows NT setup is the same as when you started. This way, your screen setup will match the illustrations in the following lessons.

Remove commands from your Start menu and Programs menus

1   Remove the Character Map command from your Start menu. (Hint: Use the right mouse button to click the taskbar, and then click Properties.)

2   Remove the Calculator command from your Programs menu.

Remove shortcuts from your Desktop

1   Remove one of your shortcuts from your Desktop using the Delete command. (Hint: Use the right mouse button to click the icon.)

2   Remove the other two shortcuts from your Desktop using Recycle Bin.

For more information on	See
Customizing your menus	Lesson 3
Customizing your display	Lesson 3

Finish the Review & Practice

1   Close all open windows by clicking the Close button in the upper-right corner of each window.

2   If any window is minimized, use the right mouse button to click the window's taskbar button, and then click Close.

You are now ready to start the next lesson, or you can work on your own.

3   If you are finished using Windows NT for now, on the Start menu, click Shut Down, and then click Yes.

Using Windows NT Accessories and Tools to Get Your Work Done

Part

2

Using WordPad to Generate Text Documents

Estimated time
40 min.

In this lesson you will learn how to:

- Create text documents using the Windows NT WordPad accessory.
- Edit WordPad documents.
- Format WordPad documents.

Although Microsoft Windows NT is the operating system that provides the environment in which you perform your computing work, it is the programs that provide the tools you use to accomplish your tasks. For example, you might use a spreadsheet program to develop budgets and perform calculations. You purchase and set up programs separately from Windows NT, but you use Windows NT to run them. The operating system handles a number of functions, such as the communication between the programs and your computer hardware, and manages your computer's memory.

Some of the most common tasks done using a computer include writing letters and reports. Using a word processing program, you can easily type letters, reports, manuscripts, and more. After a document is typed or as you are typing, you can edit the text and move sections around without having to retype a word. You can format the document to make it look more professional, as well as print it.

In Windows NT, you have a built-in word processing program, called WordPad, that you can use to create simple documents. In this lesson, you'll use WordPad to create, edit, format, and print a memo.

Creating a Document with WordPad

In a typical workday, you might need to write several documents, such as memos, letters, or reports. Although you could use a full-featured word processing program such as Microsoft Word to do these tasks, WordPad is a more than adequate substitute for small, simpler documents. With WordPad, you can perform all of the basic word processing tasks such as creating, editing, formatting, saving and printing documents.

WordPad might be sufficient if you don't typically write a large number of letters or notes. If you're considering purchasing a word processing program, using WordPad can give you a preview of some of the functions you can expect to see in such a program.

Each time you start WordPad, you see a blank screen, similar to a blank sheet of paper, on which you can write your document. When you are ready to write, simply begin typing. As you reach the end of a line, WordPad automatically breaks the line near the right margin and moves the last word to the next line as you continue typing. This feature is called *wordwrap*. You do not have to press ENTER (comparable to the carriage return key on a typewriter) to go to the next line.

Start WordPad

Suppose you want to write a company memo announcing a corporate event. In this exercise, you start the Windows NT WordPad accessory.

1   If your computer isn't already on, turn it on now. If necessary, press CTRL+ALT+DELETE to log on. Type your password if you're using one, and then press ENTER. If you see the Welcome dialog box, click the Close button.

2   Click Start. On the Start menu, point to Programs, and then point to Accessories.

3   On the Accessories menu, click WordPad.

    WordPad starts. At the top of the window are the menu bar, the toolbar, and the format bar.

Lesson 4: Using WordPad to Generate Text Documents

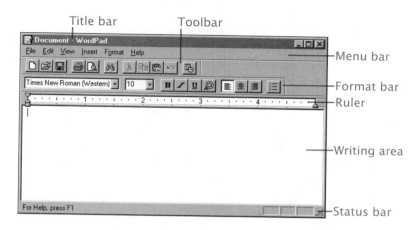

Title bar   Toolbar

Menu bar

Format bar

Ruler

Writing area

Status bar

Maximize

4   Click the Maximize button.

The WordPad window fills up the screen.

 NOTE   If you do not see one of the screen elements in your WordPad window, click the View menu and make sure that a check mark appears beside each of the four items listed: Toolbar, Format Bar, Ruler, and Status Bar. If any of these four items is not checked, click it to select it.

Enter text

You want to write a memo announcing the company picnic to all employees. In this exercise, you enter text in WordPad.

1   In the writing area of the WordPad window, type **TO: All Employees**

If you make any mistakes, you can either leave them for editing in a later exercise, or use the BACKSPACE key to erase the errors, and then type the corrections.

2   Press ENTER.

This ends the line and positions the insertion point at the beginning of a second line.

3   Type **FROM: Childs Play Management**

4   Press ENTER twice.

The first ENTER ends the "FROM" line. The second ENTER adds a blank line.

5 Now type the following text:

This month marks our 15th year of business. We will be celebrating this event with a company picnic on Friday, June 6. The picnic begins at 10:00 AM, and everyone is invited to join the fun. See you there!

If your memo did not wordwrap, on the View menu, click Options. Make sure that the Word 6 tab is active. In the Word Wrap box, click Wrap To Ruler, and then click OK.

6 Press ENTER to end the paragraph.

 NOTE When you press ENTER, you insert a hidden character called a *paragraph mark*, which indicates the end of the line followed by the start of a new paragraph.

Save a document

During the course of your work, it's a good idea to save your document from time to time. Saving the document creates a permanent file on your hard disk or floppy disk so that you can work with the document again, even after you've shut the computer down and restarted it. When you save your document, you need to give it a name that helps you identify its contents. In this exercise, you save the document you just created.

Save

1 On the toolbar, click the Save button.

The Save As dialog box appears.

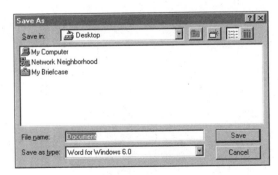

2 Under the Save In box, double-click My Computer, and then double-click the hard disk (C:).

A list of the folders stored on your hard disk appears.

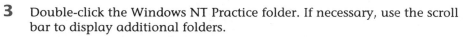

3   Double-click the Windows NT Practice folder. If necessary, use the scroll bar to display additional folders.

Your saved file will be stored in the Windows NT practice folder.

4   In the File Name box, select the word Document, type **Picnic Memo**, and then click the Save button.

In Windows NT, a filename can be up to 255 characters in length, with both uppercase and lowercase letters. You can also use spaces in the filename.

Close

5   Click the Close button to close the WordPad window.

The WordPad window containing the memo closes.

Retrieve a WordPad document

A few days after having drafted the memo, you decide to take another look at it and edit it. In this exercise, you open the memo.

1   Click Start. On the Start menu, point to Programs, and then point to Accessories.

2   On the Accessories menu, click WordPad.

WordPad starts.

Open

3   On the toolbar, click the Open button.

The Open dialog box appears.

4   Under the Look In box, double-click My Computer, and then double-click the hard disk (C:).

The contents of your hard disk appear.

5   Double-click the Windows NT Practice folder.

6   In the Files Of Type box, click the down arrow, and then click All Documents.

All files stored in the Windows NT Practice folder appear.

7   Double-click the Picnic Memo file.

Your memo opens in the WordPad window.

TIP   You can also open a document on which you have recently worked by using the Documents menu. To do this, click Start. On the Start menu, point to Documents. The Documents menu lists up to the last 15 documents you have opened in any program. Click the document name. Then, the document opens in the program with which it was created.

Making Changes to a Document

With WordPad, you can easily add, delete, and change words and characters in your document. Whenever you edit text, the first thing you do is select the text you want to modify or the area where you want to make your correction. Then, you can make changes by adding or deleting text.

You need to change the date and some wording in your memo. In the following exercises, you select, insert, replace, and delete characters and words.

Select text

Before you can edit, you need to position the insertion point or select text. In this exercise, you click and drag to select locations and text in your WordPad document.

1   Maximize the Picnic Memo window, if it is not already maximized.

2   Use your mouse to click just before the "j" in "June."

3   Use your mouse to drag across the word "June 6."

"June" is highlighted in black, indicating that it is selected. You can then start typing over and editing all the selected letters or words at once.

4   Double-click the word "celebrating."

The word "celebrating" is highlighted, indicating that it is selected.

NOTE   The area near the left edge of the WordPad window is called the *selection bar*. If you place your mouse pointer on the selection bar, it changes to an arrow pointing to the upper-right corner. Clicking the selection bar with the mouse selects the line that the mouse pointer is pointing to. Double-clicking the selection bar selects the entire paragraph the mouse pointer is pointing to, and triple-clicking the selection bar selects the entire document.

Insert text

When you place your insertion point between existing characters and start typing, the characters to the right of the insertion point move over to make room for the new characters. This is a quick and easy way for you to insert letters or spaces into your text. In this exercise, you insert additional information into your memo.

1 Use your mouse to click just before the "j" in "join the fun."

Your insertion point appears just before the "j."

2 Use the left arrow key to move left one space, and then press the SPACEBAR once.

3 Type **take a paid vacation day off and**

Your new text appears before the text already in place. The sentence now reads "The picnic begins at 10:00 AM, and everyone is invited to take a paid vacation day off and join the fun."

Replace text

Once you have selected text by dragging or clicking, you can easily type new text to replace the selection. In this exercise, you quickly replace selected text.

1 Select the words "15th year."

The words "15th year" are highlighted in black, indicating that they are selected.

2 Type **14th anniversary**

The sentence now reads "This month marks our 14th anniversary of business."

Delete text

You can delete single letters or an entire selection by pressing DELETE or BACK-SPACE. This is a convenient method for making quick corrections when entering or editing text. In this exercise, you delete characters and words.

1 In the second sentence, place the insertion point between "6" and the period.

2 Press BACKSPACE.

The number "6" is deleted.

3 Type **13** to change the date to June 13.

4 In the third sentence, click between the "1" and "0" in "10:00."

5 Press DELETE.

The number "0" is deleted.

6 Type **1** to change the time to 11:00.

7 Select the word "vacation".

8 Delete the word "vacation," and then press BACKSPACE once.

Split a paragraph

You can break a paragraph into two by inserting a paragraph mark. In this exercise, you split a paragraph into two paragraphs and add a blank line.

1 Click just before the "S" in "See you there."

2 Press ENTER.

All the text located after the insertion point moves to the next line, creating a new paragraph.

3 Press ENTER again.

All the text located after the insertion point moves to the next line, creating a blank line between the two paragraphs.

Indent paragraphs by tabbing

In this exercise, you indent the first line of the two paragraphs to make them standout.

1 With the insertion point already placed before the "S" in "See you there," press TAB.

The second paragraph is indented one-half inch.

2 Click just before the "T" in "This month marks" in the first paragraph.

3 Press TAB.

Your memo should now look similar to the following illustration.

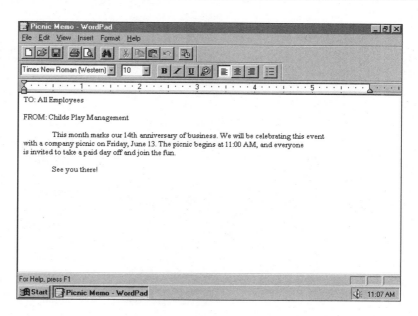

Save

4   On the toolbar, click the Save button.

A new version of the memo, that includes the edits you made, is created and saved on your hard disk.

   TIP   You can easily set additional tabs by clicking the desired locations on the ruler. If you want to control the position of the tabs more precisely, click Tabs on the Format menu.

Formatting a Document

You can change the presentation of a document to make it look more polished and professional. In the following exercises, you will change the lettering, or *font,* of the document as well as set new margins. You will be using the format bar to quickly make some of these modifications.

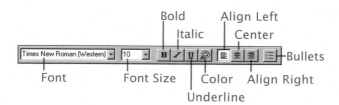

Change the font and font size

In this exercise, you use the format bar to change fonts throughout the document.

1 On the Edit menu, click Select All.

   Your entire document is selected.

2 On the format bar, open the Font box by clicking its down arrow.

   The list of fonts set up on your computer appears.

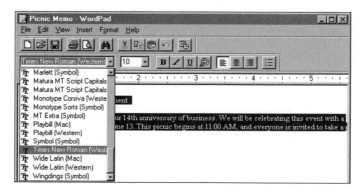

3 In the Font box, click Arial (Western).

   The Arial (Western) font is applied to all the text in your memo.

4 On the format bar, click the down arrow next to the Font Size box, and then click 14.

   The new font size is applied to all the text in your memo.

5 Select the words "paid day off," and then click the Italic button.

   The selected words change to italic style.

Italic

6 Select the "TO:" and "FROM:" memo header lines.

7 On the format bar, click the Bold button.

   The selected lines change to bold style.

Bold

8 Click anywhere in the document.

   Your memo should look similar to the following illustration.

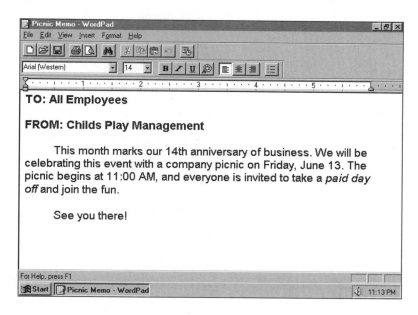

Save

9   On the toolbar, click the Save button.

Set the margins

As a finishing touch, you might want to change your margin settings as an additional way to format your memo. Changing the margin settings allows you tailor the shape of paragraphs and the amount of text that can fit on the page. In this exercise, you narrow your margins.

1   On the File menu, click Page Setup.

The Page Setup dialog box appears.

2   In the Left box, type **1.5** to specify a one-and-one-half-inch left margin.

3   In the Right box, type **1** to indicate a one-inch right margin.

The sample document reflects your change.

4   Click OK, and then click the Save button on the toolbar.

The margins of your memo change according to your specifications, although you might not see any changes in your document until you preview or print it. *Previewing* a document is a way to see what it will look like before you actually print it.

Printing a Document

Once your document is ready for distribution, you can print it. You can choose the number of copies you want to print. If your document has more than one page, you can specify the range of pages you want to print. Using the Print Preview command, you can see what your printed page will look like, including the margins and other formatting you have specified.

   NOTE   To complete the following exercises, you must have an installed printer connected to your computer. To install a printer, click Start, point to Settings, and then click Printers. Double-click Add Printer and follow the wizard directions.

Preview the printed memo

In this exercise, you preview your WordPad document to check the new margins.

Print Preview

You can also choose Print Preview on the File menu.

1   On the toolbar, click the Print Preview button.

The Print Preview window appears, showing your memo with the margin settings you specified.

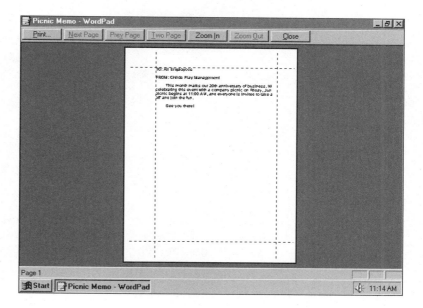

2   In the Print Preview window, click Close.

The Print Preview window closes, and the Picnic Memo-WordPad window appears again.

Print your memo

Now that you have verified that your memo looks the way you want, you can print it for distribution. In this exercise, you print the document.

1   Make sure that the printer that is connected to your computer is turned on.

2   On the File menu, click Print.

The Print dialog box appears.

83

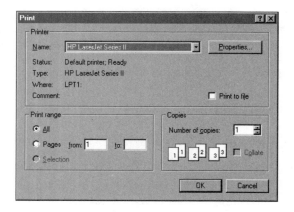

3   Click OK.

One copy of your memo is printed on your printer.

One Step Further: Creating a Template Using an Existing File

Suppose you want to make a copy of the Picnic Memo to use as a starting point for future memos. You can use the Save As command to create a *template* by saving your memo under another name and preserving the original version. In this exercise, you create a template file.

1   On the File menu, click Save As.

The Save As dialog box appears.

2   Make sure that the file is set to be saved in the Windows NT Practice folder on your hard disk (C:).

3   If the Picnic Memo filename in the File Name box is not already selected, select it.

4   Type **Winter Party Memo Template**, and then click Save.

The memo is saved on your hard disk under its new name. The other version of your document is preserved under its original name, Picnic Memo.

Finish the lesson

In the following steps, you will return your computer to the settings it had when you started this lesson. You will also close any open windows.

Restore

1   Click the Restore button in the upper-right corner of the WordPad window.

Close

2 Close all open windows by clicking the Close button in the upper-right corner of each window.

3 If any window is minimized, use the right mouse button to click the window's taskbar button, and then click Close.

You are now ready to start the next lesson, or you can work on your own.

4 If you are finished using Windows NT for now, on the Start menu, click Shut Down, and then click Yes.

Lesson Summary

To	Do this	Button
Start WordPad	On the Start menu, point to Programs, point to Accessories, and then click WordPad.	
Enter text in WordPad	In the writing area of the WordPad window, type the text you want.	
Save a WordPad document	On the toolbar, click the Save button.	🖫
View the toolbar, format bar, ruler, or status bar	On the View menu, click the item you want to view.	
Save copy of a WordPad document under a new name	On the File menu, click Save As. Specify the new filename, and then click Save.	
Open a WordPad document	On the toolbar, click the Open button. Select the location and name of the file, and then click Open.	🗁
Select multiple characters	Drag across the characters.	
Select a word	Double-click the word.	
Select several words	Double-click the first word, and drag across the additional words.	
Select a line	Click the selection bar located at the left edge of the window beside the line.	
Select a paragraph	Double-click the selection bar beside the paragraph.	
Select all text in a document	Triple-click the selection bar.	
Insert text between existing characters	Position the insertion point where you want to insert text, and then type the new text.	

To	Do this	Button
Replace existing text with new text	Select the text to be replaced by dragging or double-clicking it, and then type the new text.	
Delete a character	Use the mouse to position the insertion point, and then press DELETE to remove a character to the right of the insertion point, or press BACKSPACE to remove a character to the left of the insertion point.	
Delete several characters	Select the text to be deleted by dragging or double-clicking, and then press DELETE or BACKSPACE.	
Split a paragraph into two	Position the insertion point where you want to split the paragraph, and then press ENTER.	
Insert tabbed indents	Position the insertion point where you want to insert the tabbed indent, and then press TAB.	
Change the font	Select the text whose font you want to change. On the format bar, click a new font, font size, or font style.	
Set the margins	On the File menu, click Page Setup. In the Margins area, type the left, right, top, or bottom margin settings you want, and then click OK.	
Preview a document	On the toolbar, click Print Preview.	
Print a document	On the File menu, click Print. Make any changes you want in the Print dialog box, and then click OK.	

For online information about	In the Help Topics dialog box, click Index, and then type
Creating and editing text	**Editing,** *and then click* **Text In Short Documents**

Drawing Pictures Using Paint

Estimated time
30 min.

In this lesson you will learn how to:

- Create simple drawings using the Windows NT Paint accessory.
- Select, copy, paste, and move shapes in drawings.
- Add text and color to drawings.

Some information is best described, not in words, but in pictures. Instead of using a pencil or pen to draw on a piece of paper, you can use a computer program to draw, edit, and manipulate graphic objects. Microsoft Windows NT comes with a *paint program* accessory, called Paint, that you can use to draw graphic objects, such as lines and circles.

The width and height of a Paint drawing are expressed in *pixels*, or *pels*. Pixels are "picture elements," the smallest graphic unit that can be displayed on your screen. Pixels make up all the shapes you see on your screen, whether they are letters, lines, or circles. By using different colors, such as black or white for certain pixels, you can see the pixels form different shapes.

You can use Paint to view or draw simple graphics. In this lesson, you'll use Paint to create, manipulate, color, and print a drawing.

Creating a Simple Picture with Paint

Using the Paint accessory, you can draw simple pictures, logos, maps, and symbols. You can also create, edit, move, and size a drawing, as well as print it and save it on your disk for later use.

If you don't typically create or view many graphics, and therefore don't need the services of a full-featured drawing program, Paint might answer your needs.

When you start Paint, you see a blank screen, which is like a blank sheet of paper on which you can draw your graphic. A *toolbox* containing the tools that you use to create your drawing is located on the left side of the window. A *color box* from which you select the colors for the different parts of your drawing is located at the bottom of the window.

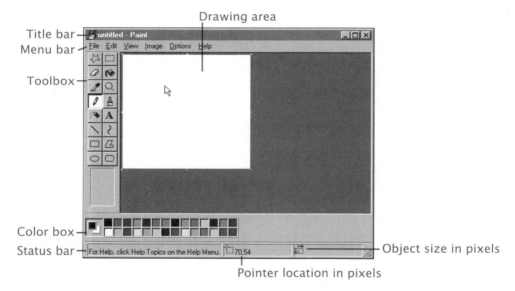

The toolbox includes the tools available to draw shapes, color areas, select shapes, add text, edit lines, and more. The following illustration shows the names of all the drawing tools available on the toolbox.

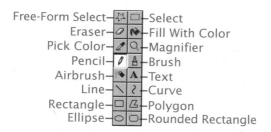

Free-Form Select—|Select
Eraser—|Fill With Color
Pick Color—|Magnifier
Pencil—|Brush
Airbrush—|Text
Line—|Curve
Rectangle—|Polygon
Ellipse—|Rounded Rectangle

In the following exercises, you'll be working on a product logo concept for Childs Play's new preschool product line. You'll use Paint to create a drawing for this product line. When you've finished, your logo will look similar to the following illustration.

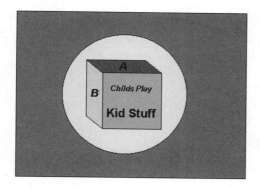

Start Paint

In this exercise, you start the Windows NT Paint accessory.

1 If your computer isn't already on, turn it on now. If necessary, press CTRL+ALT+DELETE to log on. Type your password if you're using one, and then press ENTER. If you see the Welcome dialog box, click the Close button.

2 Click Start. On the Start menu, point to Programs, and then point to Accessories.

3 On the Accessories menu, click Paint.

4 Maximize the Paint window by clicking the Maximize button.

Maximize

Set the drawing size

In this exercise, you set the drawing size, the first step in creating your new logo. The attributes you set will apply to this and all future drawings, until you change the attributes again.

1   On the Image menu, click Attributes.

The Attributes dialog box appears.

2   In the Units area, click the Inches option button.

The unit used to measure the width and the height of the drawing changes to inches.

3   Double-click the number in the Width box, and then type **4**

4   Press TAB, and then type **3** in the Height box.

5   Click OK.

The drawing area is now 4 inches wide and 3 inches tall.

 TIP   By default, the drawing image area is 640x480 pixels, or approximately 6.67x5 inches. If you want to return to the default (or original) drawing size, in the Attributes dialog box, click Default.

Draw a simple shape

In this exercise, you use Paint to draw a square.

Rectangle

1   Click the Rectangle tool.

2   Hold down SHIFT and drag from the upper-left corner to the lower-right corner to draw a perfect square.

The size of any shape you draw appears in the status area and is measured in pixels.

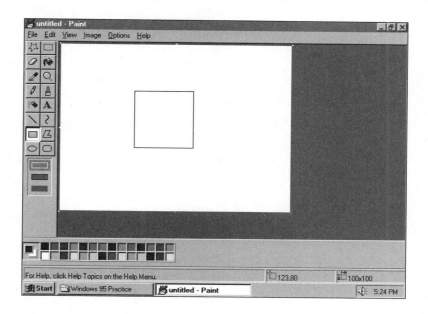

Select, copy, paste, and move shapes

In this exercise, you select the graphic objects you want and duplicate them in your drawing.

Select

1   Click the Select tool.

2   Place the mouse pointer just above the upper-left corner of the square, and drag diagonally just beyond the lower-right corner.

A dotted line appears around your square, indicating that the square is selected for further editing.

3   On the Edit menu, click Copy.

The square is copied in the computer's memory.

4   On the Edit menu, click Paste.

The contents of your copied selection appear in the upper-left corner of your drawing area.

5   Drag the pasted square in front of your original square, as shown in the following illustration.

91

Opaque

6 Below the toolbox, click the Opaque option which is the first of the two options displayed.

7 Click anywhere in the drawing area to permanently place the top square.

Your screen should look similar to the following illustration.

Draw lines

In this exercise, you connect two squares with a line.

Line

1 Click the Line tool.

2 In the drawing area, drag from the upper-left corner of one square to the upper-left corner of the other square. Use the crosshairs mouse pointer to help you position the line precisely.

A line connects the two rectangles.

3 Drag a line between the two upper-right corners of the squares.

4 Drag a line between the two lower-left corners of the squares.

The two squares are connected, creating a cube.

Save your drawing

In this exercise, you name and save your new drawing.

1 On the File menu, click Save.

The Save As dialog box appears.

2 In the Save In box, double-click My Computer, and then double-click the hard disk (C:).

3 Double-click the Windows NT Practice folder. Use the scroll bar if necessary.

4 Double-click in the File Name box, and then type **Preschool Toys Logo**.

5 Click Save.

The file is saved in your Windows NT Practice folder.

Magnify and edit your graphic

You want to make your graphic look more like a child's toy block. In this exercise, you erase extra lines from the block.

Magnifier

1 Click the Magnifier tool.

2 In the drawing area, click over the lower-left corner of the cube using the magnification rectangle.

The part of the drawing you clicked on is magnified.

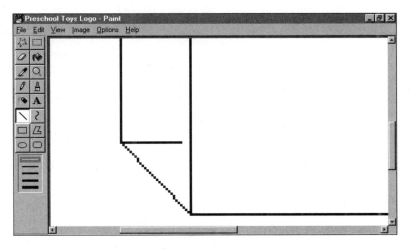

Eraser

3 Click the Eraser tool.

93

4 Drag the Eraser tool over the extra horizontal line on the back square.

The line is erased. If you accidentally erase too much, on the Edit menu, click Undo, and then try again.

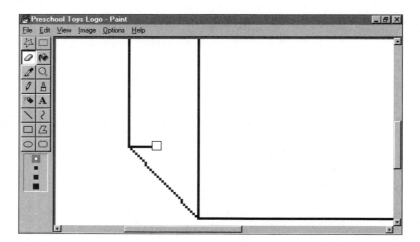

5 Click the Magnifier tool again, and then click anywhere in the drawing area.

The drawing returns to its original size.

6 Click the Magnifier tool, and then click over the upper-right corner of the block.

The part of the drawing you clicked on is magnified.

7 Drag the Eraser tool over the extra vertical line of the back square until it is erased.

8 Click the Magnifier tool, and then click anywhere in the drawing area.

The drawing returns to its original size. Your block should look similar to the following illustration.

9 On the File menu, click Save.

Draw a circle

In this exercise, you draw a circle around the cube.

Ellipse

1   Click the Ellipse tool.

2   Hold down SHIFT and drag from above the upper-left corner to beyond the lower-right corner of the cube to draw a perfect circle.

3   When the circle is the size you want, release the mouse button, and then release the SHIFT key.

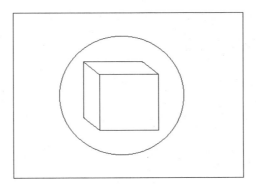

4   On the File menu, click Save.

Adding Text to a Picture

Adding text to your graphic is like adding any other graphic element, and consists of two parts. First, you define the *text block*, the area where you want the text to appear. Then, you type the text you want in it. You can also change the font and size of the text.

Unlike WordPad, Paint does not support *wordwrap*, so you must press ENTER at the end of each line. You can edit your text with the BACKSPACE key or by positioning the insertion point. Once the text is in place, it behaves just like any other graphic element. You can change its color or position using tools from the toolbox, but the only way to edit its content is to delete the text block and create a new one.

Add text to a graphic

In this exercise, you add the first two letters of the alphabet and the text of the logo to the toy block drawing.

Text

1   In the toolbox, click the Text tool.

2   In the drawing, drag a square inside the top center of the cube to define the text block.

95

An insertion point appears in the text area, and the Text toolbar appears at the top of the window.

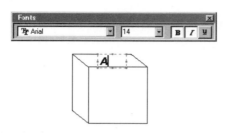

3 In the text area, type **A**

4 In the Text toolbar, select the Arial (Western) font, 14 point size, Bold, and Italic.

The text is formatted according to your specifications.

Transparent

5 Click the Transparent option.

Select

6 If the "A" is not positioned correctly, click the Select tool, draw a selection box around the "A," and then move the letter by dragging it.

7 Repeat steps 2 through 6 to place the letter "B" on the left side of the block.

Text

8 On the top half of the front of the block, use the Text tool to create a text area, and then type **Childs Play** in 10-point Arial bold italic.

9 Click the Text tool again, and on the lower half of the front of the block, type **Kid Stuff** in 16-point Arial bold.

Changing Colors in a Picture

You can add colors to your drawing. This can be especially useful if you use a color printer or if you plan on sending your drawing online, for example, by sending it in a piece of e-mail. If you're using a black-and-white printer, the colors appear on your screen, and are reproduced in different shades of gray on your printed page.

Add color to your drawing

In this exercise, you color the different areas of your drawing.

1 On the color box, click any shade of green you want.

2 Click the Fill With Color tool.

3 Click the front of the block.

Fill With Color

The front face of the block is filled with the color green.

4 Repeat steps 1 through 3 to fill the other areas of the graphic with the different colors.

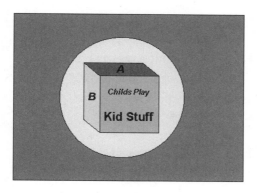

Line

Curve

Magnifier

If a section of the graphic is filled with a color you did not intend, this might mean that a graphic object is not completely enclosed. When there are open lines in a graphic object, the color "leaks" out into other objects. You can repair broken lines by connecting them with the Line or Curve tool.

5   On the File menu, click Save.

 TIP   If you want, you can also color the open spaces within letters. Click the Magnifier tool, and then click the character you want to magnify and fill with color. Click the color you want, click the Fill With Color tool, and then click the open space in the letter. Repeat this process for all letters that need to be filled with color.

Printing a Picture

You can preview your drawings online, including their margins, formatting, and position before printing them. Once your drawings look the way you want, you can define the number of copies you need, and then print them.

Preview your printed drawing

You have finished drawing your graphic, and are now ready to print it out. But first, you want to check the drawing's position on the page. In this exercise, you preview your Paint document.

 IMPORTANT   To use Print Preview in this exercise, you must have a printer installed.

1   On the File menu, click Print Preview.

     The Print Preview window appears, showing a picture of your graphic, including its size and position on the page.

2   In the Print Preview window, click Close.

     The Paint window appears again.

Print your drawing

You now want to print the drawing to have it reviewed by the Advertising department for further development and refinement. In this exercise, you print the drawing.

 NOTE   If your computer is not connected to a printer, skip this exercise. For more information about installing a printer, see Appendix A.

---

1   Turn on the printer that is connected to your computer.

2   On the File menu, click Print.

     The Print dialog box appears.

3   Click OK.

     Your drawing is printed.

One Step Further: Creating a New Desktop Background

Now that you have learned how to use Paint, use your newly acquired skills to create a new drawing. Assume that you work in the Marketing Department of Childs Play, Inc. You are asked to create a graphic that will be included in one of the new marketing pieces.

Create a new drawing

1   On the File menu, click New.

     The Preschool Toys Logo disappears and is replaced with a blank drawing area.

2   On the toolbox, click the Ellipse tool.

3   Below the toolbox, click the filled and outlined shape which is the second of the three options.

Ellipse

4 Draw three overlapping ovals that look like a group of balloons.

5 Fill each oval with a different color.

Pencil

6 Use the Pencil tool to draw strings that appear to dangle from each balloon.

Your picture should look similar to the following illustration.

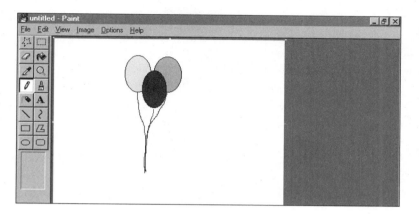

7 Add a text block below the balloons, and then type **Childs Play—We're Taking Off!**

8 Format the text as 12-point Times New Roman bold.

9 Save the file in your Windows NT Practice folder as Balloons Graphic.

10 Minimize the Print window.

Use your drawing as the background of your Desktop

You like the drawing that you just created so much that you decide to use it as the background for your Desktop. In this exercise, you apply the newly created drawing to your background.

1 On the Start menu, point to Settings, and then click Control Panel.

2 Double-click Display. Make sure that the Background tab is active.

3 Under Wallpaper, click the Browse button.

The Browse dialog box appears.

4 Locate the Windows NT Practice folder, and then click the Balloons Graphic file.

5 Click Open.

Windows NT displays a preview of the new background using the Balloons Graphic file.

Close

6 Click OK, and then click the Close button to close the Control Panel window.

The Balloons Graphic file is displayed as the background for your Desktop.

Remove the drawing from the background of your Desktop

After a few hours, you find that the Balloons Graphic is distracting, and you decide to restore your original wallpaper. In this exercise, you remove the drawing from the background of your Desktop.

1 On the Start menu, point to Settings, and then click Control Panel.

2 Double-click Display, and then make sure that the Background tab is active.

3 Under Wallpaper, click None.

4 Click OK, and then click the Close button to close the Control Panel window.

The Balloons Graphic file is removed from the background of your Desktop.

Finish the lesson

In the following steps, you will return your computer to the settings it had when you started this lesson. You will also close any open windows.

1 Use the right mouse button to click the Paint button on the taskbar, and on the shortcut menu, click Close. Close any other open windows.

You are now ready to start the next lesson, or you can work on your own.

2 If you are finished using Windows NT for now, on the Start menu, click Shut Down, and then click Yes.

Lesson Summary

To	Do this	Button
Start Paint	On the Start menu, point to Programs, point to Accessories, and then click Paint.	
Draw a simple shape	Click the tool for the shape you want to draw, and then drag the shape in the drawing area.	

To	Do this	Button
Select a portion of your drawing	Click the Select tool, and then drag across the area you want to select.	
Copy and paste a portion of your drawing	Use the Select tool to select the portion you want to copy. On the Edit menu, click Copy. Place the insertion where you want to insert the copied drawing, and then click Paste on the Edit menu.	
Move a portion of your drawing	Use the Select tool to select the portion you want to move, and then drag it to its new location.	
Magnify a portion of your drawing	Click the Magnifier tool, and then click over the area you want to magnify.	
Erase a portion of your drawing	Click the Eraser tool, and then drag the tool over the area you want to erase.	
Add text to the drawing	Click the Text tool, and then drag across to create a text block. Type the desired text.	
Add color to the drawing	Click the color you want, and then draw lines, or click the shape, and click the Fill With Color Tool.	
Save your drawing	On the File menu, click Save. In the Save dialog box, specify the disk drive, folder, and filename, and then click Save.	
Print your drawing	On the File menu, click Print. In the Print dialog box, click OK.	

For online information about	In the Help Topics dialog box, click Index, and then type
Creating, editing, and viewing drawings using Paint	**Paint**

Using Programs and Accessories To Do Your Work

In this lesson you will learn how to:

- Locate and start Windows NT-based and MS-DOS–based programs.
- Switch between open programs.
- Share information between different programs.

Estimated time
35 min.

In your day to day work, you will likely be required to use supplies and resources that are more specialized and specific than the generic tools, such as a fax machine, a notepad, or a briefcase. Similarly with Windows NT, you will likely be required to use specialized programs to help you perform specific types of tasks, such as word processing or project management, in addition to the basic accessories, such as WordPad and Paint. You must acquire these programs separately—they do not come with Windows NT. However, Windows NT provides the foundation for and the environment in which these programs can operate. In this lesson, you'll learn how to locate and start the different programs that are set up on your computer. You'll also learn how to switch between multiple open programs and how to share information between them.

Starting Windows NT-Based Programs

It's likely that you'll need to use programs, besides the Windows NT accessories, to do some of your work. You'll probably buy the programs you need from a computer store, catalog, or other resource, and then set them up on your computer. Examples of such programs include Microsoft Access (a database program), Microsoft Word (a word processing program), or Microsoft Publisher (a graphics program).

Regardless of the type of program, Windows NT-based programs have certain elements and characteristics in common. The following illustration shows a few Windows NT-based programs open on your Desktop.

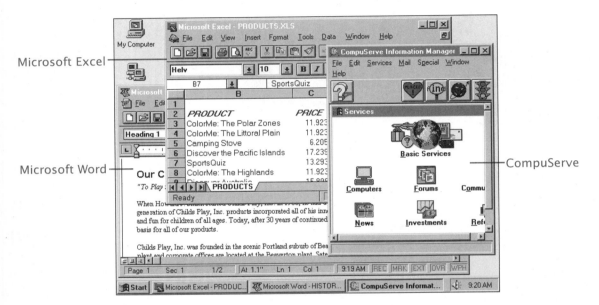

When a program opens in its window, you see the familiar window controls, including the Minimize, Maximize, and Close buttons. If the contents of the window extend beyond the window's boundaries, you'll also see the horizontal and vertical scroll bars.

Each Windows NT-based program has a menu bar across the top of its window, from which you can choose commands to control the program. Many programs also use one or more toolbars, on which you can click a button that acts as a command shortcut.

To start a Windows NT-based program, you can browse through My Computer or Windows NT Explorer to find the program file, and then double-click the filename. If you're not sure what a program file looks like, you can tell by viewing the file extensions. In order to display this kind of information, you might need to turn this option on in Windows NT Explorer or My Computer. Program files have an .EXE file extension. When you upgrade to Microsoft Windows NT Workstation, your existing programs are automatically added to the Programs menu on the Start menu. Similarly, when you install a new program, it is by default added to the Programs menu. If you prefer, you can also create a Desktop shortcut to any program to run them by simply clicking an icon.

In the following exercises, you'll locate and start a program using two different methods.

Browse through My Computer to start a program

Suppose you have set up a new software program on your computer's hard disk, and are now ready to run it. In this exercise, you browse through your files to find and start the program.

1   If your computer isn't already on, turn it on now. If necessary, press CTRL+ALT+DELETE to log on. Type your password if you're using one, and then press ENTER. If you see the Welcome dialog box, click the Close button.

2   Double-click the My Computer icon.

3   Double-click the hard disk (C:) icon.

4   Double-click the Windows NT Practice folder.

5   Double-click the Quotes folder.

For more information on finding files, see Lesson 8.

The Quotes folder contains a program named Quotables, along with a text file. If you're not sure which one is the Quotables program file, you can tell by viewing the file extensions. On the View menu, click Options, and then click the View tab. Click the Show All Files option button, and click OK. The Quotables file has an .EXE file extension.

Quotables

6   Double-click the Quotables program file icon.

The Quotables program starts, and displays the text of a famous quote. Although the quote might be different, your screen should look similar to the following illustration.

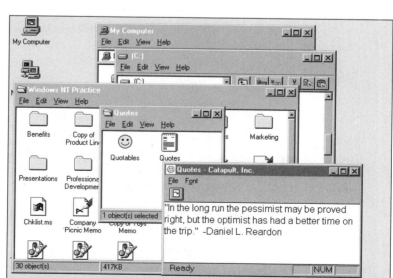

105

Next Quote

Close

7 Click the Next Quote button.

The next quotation appears.

8 Click the Close button to close the window and shut down the Quotables program.

Use the Find command to start a program

Suppose you know that you have a type of quotation program on your hard disk, but you don't know where it is located or what its exact name is. In this exercise, you find and start a program using the Find command.

1 Click Start. On the Start menu, point to Find, and then click Files Or Folders.

The Find dialog box appears. Be sure that the Name & Location tab is active.

2 In the Named box, type **quot**

You use the fact that you know the program has "quot" somewhere in its name to narrow the search.

3 Click the Advanced tab.

4 Click the Of Type down arrow.

A list of all available file types appear.

When you specify the Application file type, only program files are found. For more information on finding files, see Lesson 8.

5 Click Application.

6 Click the Find Now button.

A list of program files that meet the criteria you defined appear at the bottom of the dialog box.

7 Double-click the Quotables program file in the Find list.

The Quotables program file starts.

8 Close the Quotables window.

Create a shortcut to start a program

Suppose you use the Quotables program frequently and want to access it quickly. In this exercise, you make the Quotables program more readily available by creating a shortcut to it on your Desktop.

1 With the Find dialog box still open, use the right mouse button to drag the Quotables program file to any empty area on your Desktop.

A shortcut menu appears.

2 Click Create Shortcut(s) Here.

An icon named "Shortcut To Quotables" appears on your Desktop.

3   Close all open windows.

4   Double-click the Shortcut To Quotables icon.

The Quotables program starts.

5   Close the Quotables window.

Running an MS-DOS–Based Program

You can use the MS-DOS Prompt command on the Programs menu to open an MS-DOS window in which you can run your MS-DOS–based programs. In the following exercises, you'll setup your MS-DOS work environment and start an MS-DOS–based program.

Open and adjust your MS-DOS window

In this exercise, you open and change the layout and size of an MS-DOS window.

1   Click Start. On the Start menu, point to Programs.

2   On the Programs menu, click Command Prompt.

An MS-DOS window opens. Command Prompt appears as a button on the taskbar. Your screen should look similar to the following illustration.

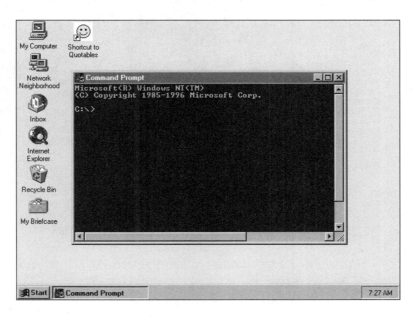

3   Drag the Command Prompt title bar to move the window to a different location on your Desktop.

Maximize

Restore

4 Click the Maximize button to switch to full-screen mode.

The MS-DOS window fills up the entire screen.

5 Click the Restore button to restore the MS-DOS window to its previous size and position on the Windows NT Desktop.

Start MS-DOS–based programs

When you work in an MS-DOS environment, you use a set of MS-DOS commands to perform actions such as displaying a list of files or changing folders. In this exercise, you type MS-DOS commands to start MS-DOS–based programs.

For more information on using MS-DOS–based programs, see Appendix C.

1 Be sure that the MS-DOS window is active. At the MS-DOS prompt (C:\), type **dir**, and then press ENTER.

The files and folders stored in the open folder on your hard disk appear in a list.

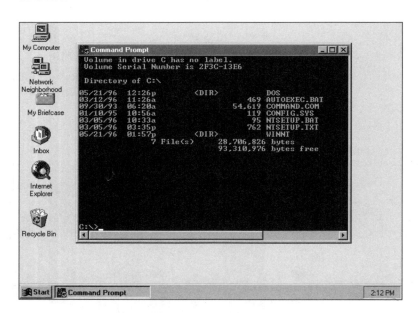

2 At the next MS-DOS prompt, type **cd "Windows NT Practice"** and then press ENTER.

The folder changes to the Windows NT Practice folder.

3 At the MS-DOS prompt (C:\Windows NT Practice), type **dir**, and then press ENTER.

A list of files and folders appears, displaying the contents of your Windows NT Practice folder.

4   At the MS-DOS prompt, type **sheet**, and then press ENTER.

The SHEET program appears. In this case, typing the name of the program starts the program itself. If you're unsure how to start an MS-DOS–based program, check its documentation.

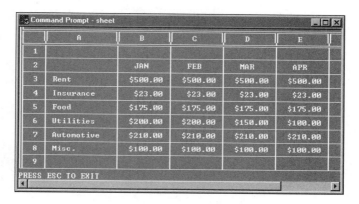

5   Click Start. On the Start menu, point to Programs, and then click Command Prompt.

A second MS-DOS window opens on your Desktop, as shown in the following illustration.

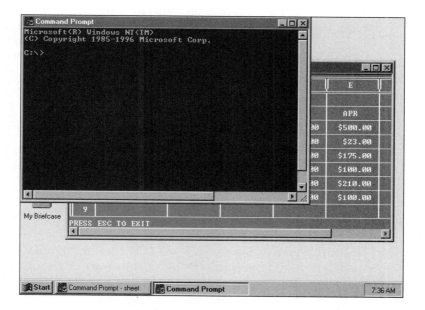

6   At the MS-DOS prompt, type **cd "Windows NT Practice"** and then press ENTER.

The folder changes to the Windows NT Practice folder.

7   At the next MS-DOS prompt, type **db**, and then press ENTER.

A display of a sample database appears. You are now running two MS-DOS–based programs at once.

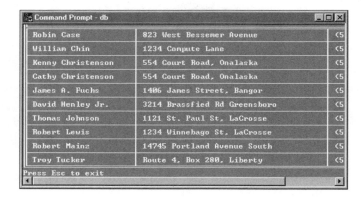

8   Press ESC.

The DB program ends, and the MS-DOS prompt appears again. Pressing the ESC key is not a standard way of quitting MS-DOS–based programs. You usually quit the program in the same way you do with Windows NT-based programs: you use the Quit or Exit command on the File menu. For more information on a particular MS-DOS–based program, check its documentation.

9   At the MS-DOS prompt, type **exit**, and then press ENTER.

The MS-DOS window closes.

10   Click the other MS-DOS window running the SHEET program to make it active.

11   Repeat steps 8 and 9 to close the SHEET program and the MS-DOS window.

Customizing Your MS-DOS Window

You can easily customize your MS-DOS window to make it suit your display preferences and the requirements of your work environment.

Change the screen size of your MS-DOS window

You can change the size of your MS-DOS window so that part of your Desktop is still visible when an MS-DOS window is open.

1   Click Start. On the Start menu, point to Programs, and then click Command Prompt.

    The Command Prompt window appears.

2   Use the right mouse button to click the title bar of the Command Prompt window, and then click Properties on the shortcut menu.

3   Click the Layout tab.

4   Under Window Size, change the Width to 50 and the Height to 15.

    The width and height refer to the number of characters wide and high the window can show at one time. So, in this case, the window size will hold 50 characters across and 15 characters high.

5   Click OK.

6   In the Apply Properties To Shortcut window, click the Modify Shortcut Which Started This Window option button.

    Subsequently, each time you click Command Prompt on the Programs menu, Microsoft Windows NT will automatically display the window at this size.

7   Click OK.

    Windows NT changes the size of the Command Prompt window.

Start your MS-DOS window so that it's full-screen size

For more information on running MS-DOS–based programs, see Appendix C.

You can set the screen size of your MS-DOS window so that it automatically fills the entire screen. This is important because some MS-DOS–based programs only run in a MS-DOS window when it is full-screen size. If your MS-DOS–based program doesn't run the way you expect it to, you can try changing the MS-DOS window so that it's full screen size.

1   Use the right mouse button to click the title bar of the Command Prompt window, and then click Properties on the shortcut menu.

2   Be sure that the Options tab is active.

3   Under Display Options, click the Full Screen option button.

4   Click OK.

5   In the Apply Properties To Shortcut window, verify that the Apply Properties To Current Window Only option button is selected.

6   Click OK.

    The MS-DOS window fills the entire screen.

7   Type **exit**

    The MS-DOS window closes.

Change the font or font size of your text, or the background color of your MS-DOS window

1   Click Start. On the Start menu, point to Programs, and then click Command Prompt.

    The Command Prompt window appears.

2   Use the right mouse button to click the title bar of the Command Prompt window, and then click Properties on the shortcut menu.

3   Click the Font tab.

4   Under Font, select the font you want to use for your MS-DOS window.

5   Under Size, select the size you want.

    Windows NT displays a sample of how the font used in the window will look.

6   Click the Colors tab.

7   Click the Screen Text option button, and then click the color you want.

8   Click Screen Background, and then click the color you want.

9   Click OK.

10 In the Apply Properties To Shortcut window, specify whether you want your changes to apply only to the current window or to all future instances of the window.

11 Click OK.

12 Type **exit**

Switching Among Multiple Open Programs

When working at your desk, you probably have several documents or project folders open at one time. While you might be actively using one, you know you can reach for and refer to other folders or documents at any time.

Similarly, you can use Windows NT to keep several programs open at the same time, each one running in its own window on your Desktop. While one window is always active and visible, you can always quickly switch to and work in any of the other windows.

Suppose you've just created a drawing in Paint and you need to write a memo to accompany the drawing. While writing your memo, you find you need to make some calculations. In the following exercises, you'll switch between Paint, WordPad, and Calculator.

Switch between programs using the taskbar

In this exercise, you write a memo to accompany your drawing.

1   Click Start. Point to Programs, point to Accessories, and then click Paint.

Paint starts.

2   On the File menu, click Open.

The Open dialog box appears.

3   In the Look In box, click My Computer, and then double-click the hard disk (C:).

The contents of your hard disk appear.

4   Double-click the Windows NT Practice folder.

The contents of the Windows NT Practice folder appear.

5   Double-click Toys Logo.

The Toys Logo drawing opens in the Paint window.

6   Click Start again. Point to Programs, point to Accessories, and then click WordPad.

WordPad starts.

7   In WordPad, type the following note.

TO: Gwen Lehua, Advertising

FROM: Craig Armand, Marketing

Attached is a logo concept I sketched for our new preschool product line. Please develop the logo based on these ideas. Note that we are working on a budget of

You now need to make a calculation of your budget.

8   Click Start. Point to Programs, point to Accessories, and then click Calculator. Enter the number 10,000 and multiply it by 2.

Switch between programs using the keyboard

You can easily switch to a program using the keyboard. In this exercise, you switch between Paint, WordPad, and Calculator using the keyboard.

1   Click the WordPad window.

2   Hold down ALT and press TAB. Do not release ALT yet.

A dialog box appears in the center of the screen, with icons that represent each of your open windows. The selected window is named at the bottom of the window and surrounded by a frame.

3 Continue to hold down ALT and press TAB repeatedly until the Paint icon is selected, and then release the ALT key.

The Paint window becomes the active window.

NOTE Pressing ALT+ESC switches, in sequence, between items listed on the taskbar. If the item is currently open, it brings its window to the top of the Desktop. If the item is currently minimized, it selects its name on the taskbar. You can then display the minimized item by pressing ENTER.

Arrange windows on the Desktop

You might need to have both the WordPad and the Calculator windows visible at the same time. In this exercise, you arrange, or *tile*, the two program windows side by side, and arrange your windows in a cascading fashion.

1 Minimize the Paint window.

2 Minimize any other windows that might be open on the Desktop except the WordPad and the Calculator windows.

3 Use the right mouse button to click an empty space on the taskbar.

A shortcut menu appears, listing commands available for arranging the open windows on the Desktop.

4 On the shortcut menu, click Tile Windows Vertically.

The two open windows are arranged side by side on your Desktop.

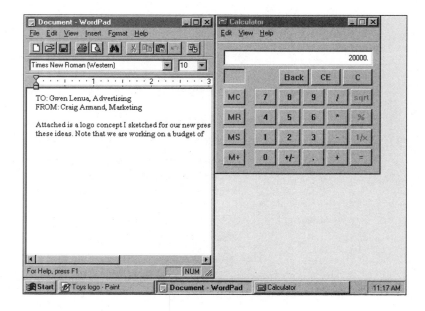

5   On the taskbar, click the Toys Logo-Paint button.

The Paint window appears on the Desktop.

6   Use the right mouse button to click an empty space on the taskbar.

7   On the shortcut menu, click Cascade Windows.

The three open windows are arranged in a cascading fashion across your Desktop. You can see each window's title bar.

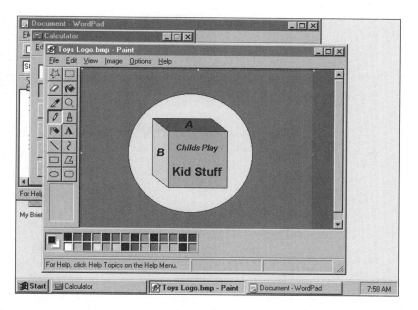

8   Close all open windows.

Sharing Information Between Different Programs

You have probably worked with paper documents in which one document had information you wanted to include in another. To avoid the inconvenience of copying by hand, you might have used scissors to cut information from one document, and then use tape or paste to place that information in another document.

In Windows NT, you can electronically cut or copy information from one program, and then paste it into another program, for example, from Paint to WordPad, or from Microsoft Excel to Microsoft Word.

Locate and open documents

You want to take a look at two documents to verify that their presentation and their contents are still up-to-date. In this exercise, you open the map drawing in Paint and the picnic memo in WordPad.

1 Double-click the My Computer icon.

The My Computer window opens.

2 Double-click the hard disk (C:) icon.

The hard disk (C:) window opens.

3 Double-click the Windows NT Practice folder.

The Windows NT Practice folder opens.

4 Double-click the Company Picnic Memo file.

The Company Picnic Memo file opens in a WordPad window.

5 On the taskbar, click the Windows NT Practice folder button.

6 In the Windows NT Practice folder, double-click the Map For Picnic file.

The Map For Picnic file opens in a Paint window.

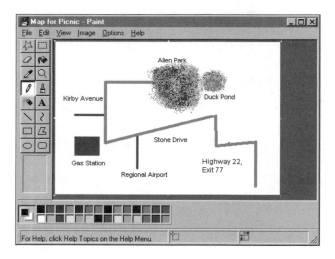

7 Maximize the Paint window.

Copy and paste information between programs

Now that you have verified that the information contained in both documents is correct, you finish the drafting of your memo by including the map to the picnic site drawing into the WordPad document. In this exercise, you copy the map and paste it into your picnic memo.

Select

1 In Paint, click the Select tool.

2 Use the Select tool to drag a dotted rectangle around the entire map.

3 On the Edit menu, click Copy.

Although nothing appears to change on your screen, the map is temporarily copied into the Clipboard, a the temporary holding place for items that have been cut or copied.

4 On the taskbar, click the Company Picnic Memo–WordPad button.

The WordPad window appears.

5 Maximize the Company Picnic Memo–WordPad window.

6 Place the mouse pointer at the end of the document, after "See you there!" and then press ENTER twice to add two blank lines.

7 On the WordPad toolbar, click the Paste button.

The map drawing is pasted in the memo.

Paste

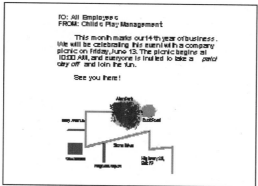

8 On the WordPad toolbar, click the Save button.

Save

Print the document containing pasted information

Now that you have finished composing your memo, you are ready to print it. In this exercise, you print the memo containing the map drawing you just pasted.

1 Be sure that your printer is on.

If you do not have a printer that can print graphics, skip to step 3.

2 On the WordPad toolbar, click the Print button.

The memo, with the inserted map, prints.

Print

3 Click the Restore button on the WordPad window.

Restore

4 Click the Restore button on the Paint window.

5 Close all open windows.

One Step Further: Embedding and Updating a Graphic That Is Part of a Memo

You can use Windows NT to insert, or *embed*, a copy of an object created in a program (the *source* program) into a document opened in another program (the *destination* program). A pasted object, like the map in the previous series of exercises, cannot be edited after it has been pasted in the new application. When you embed an object, on the other hand, the OLE technology built into Windows NT lets you use the resources of the source program to edit the embedded object without leaving the program you are currently using.

In the following exercises, you will create a new memo, embed an existing Paint drawing into the memo, and then update the embedded drawing.

Create a new WordPad document

You can embed an object into a new or existing WordPad document, as well as in many other Windows NT-based programs. In this exercise, you create a memo, in which you include an embedded drawing, that will be printed and distributed for review to your work team.

1   Click Start. On the Start menu, point to Programs, point to Accessories, and then click WordPad.

    WordPad starts.

2   Maximize the WordPad window.

3   Type the following text into the WordPad writing area.

    TO: Richard Tashi, Larry Bouldrey, Sandra Hutson

    FROM: Craig Armand

    This is the rough logo concept for our new preschool product line. I have sent this idea to Advertising for further development and refinement.

    Let me know if you have any comments or suggestions.

    Thank you.

Save

4   On the toolbar, click the Save button.

    The Save As dialog box appears. Be sure that your hard disk and the Windows NT Practice folder are selected.

5   Double-click the contents of the File Name box, type **Logo Review Memo**, and then click Save.

Embed a Paint drawing into your WordPad document

Now that you have created the WordPad memo, you're ready to insert the logo into it. In this exercise, you embed an existing drawing into your WordPad memo.

1 Press ENTER three times to move the insertion point downward and add three blank lines.

2 On the Insert menu, click Object.

The Insert Object dialog box appears with the Create New option button selected.

3 Click the Create From File option button.

4 Click Browse.

The Browse dialog box appears. Be sure that your hard disk and the Windows NT Practice folder are selected.

5 Click Toys Logo, and then click Open.

The Insert Object dialog box appears again, with the path and Toys Logo filename inserted into the File box.

6 Click OK.

The Toys Logo drawing appears in your memo. Your screen should look similar to the following illustration.

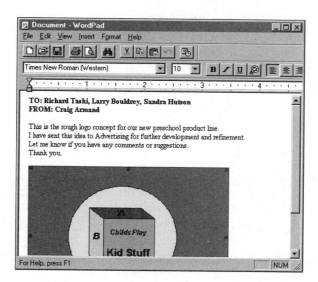

7 Click anywhere outside the Paint object window.

WordPad redraws the document.

8 On the toolbar, click the Save button.

Update the embedded drawing

You need to make some slight modifications to your drawing, and want to make sure that the most current version is included in your WordPad memo. In this exercise, you open the embedded Paint drawing and edit it, using the resources of the Paint accessory, without leaving WordPad.

1 Double-click the embedded logo drawing in the memo.

The WordPad menus and toolbars are temporarily replaced with the Paint menus, toolbox, and color box.

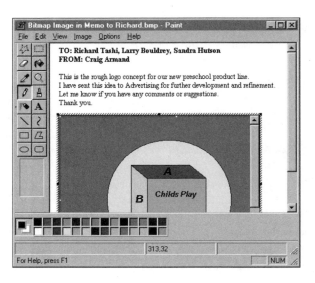

Line

2 Click the Line tool.

3 Drag several lines from any point of the circle outward toward the edge of the drawing area to simulate rays of sunshine.

The drawing should look similar to the following illustration.

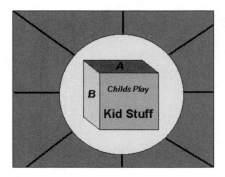

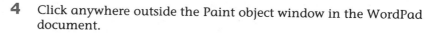

4   Click anywhere outside the Paint object window in the WordPad document.

The WordPad menu and toolbars reappear. The changes you made in Paint are reflected in the Paint logo in your memo; they are also saved in the original Toys Logo file.

5   On the WordPad toolbar, click the Save button.

6   On the WordPad window, click the Restore button.

Save

Finish the lesson

Restore

1   Close all open windows by clicking the Close button in the upper-right corner of each window.

Close

2   If any window is minimized, use the right mouse button to click the window's taskbar button, and then click Close.

3   Delete the Shortcut To Quotables shortcut from the Desktop by dragging it to the Recycle Bin or by clicking it, pressing DELETE, and then clicking Yes.

You are now ready to start the next lesson, or to work on your own.

4   If you are finished using Windows NT for now, on the Start menu, click Shut Down, and then click Yes.

Lesson Summary

To	Do this
Start and use Windows NT accessories	On the Start menu, point to Programs, and then point to Accessories. Click the accessory you want to start.
Find a program by browsing	Browse through files using Windows Explorer. Program files have an .EXE file extension. In order to display the file extension, click the View menu. Click Options, and then click the View tab. Click the Show All Files option button, and then click OK.
Find a program with Find File	Click Start, point to Find, and then click Files or Folders. Click the Advanced tab. In the Of Type box, click Application. Click Find Now. All program files located on the hard disk are found and listed.

To	Do this
Start a program	Double-click the program filename or icon.
Switch between open programs	Click the program name on the taskbar.
Tile open windows on the Desktop	Use the right mouse button to click an empty space on the taskbar. On the shortcut menu, click Tile Windows Vertically or Tile Windows Horizontally.
Cascade open windows on the Desktop	Use the right mouse button to click an empty space on the taskbar. On the shortcut menu, click Cascade Windows.
Copy and paste information between different programs	Use the Copy command to copy the information in the source program. Switch to the destination program, and then use the destinations program's Paste command to paste the information in the location you want.
Embed a Paint drawing into a WordPad document	On the WordPad Insert menu, click Object. Click the Create New or Insert From File option button. Click the object type, and then click OK.

For online information about	From the Help Topics dialog box, click Index, and then type
Opening and using the Windows NT accessories	*the accessory name*
Locating program files	**programs, finding**
Switching between different open programs	**switching, between running programs**
Copying and pasting information between different programs	**copying, information from one document to another**
Embedding information between different programs	**embedding information in documents** *or* **OLE**

Review & Practice

You will review and practice how to:

Estimated time
25 min.

- Start Windows NT accessories.
- Create a text document using WordPad.
- Create a drawing using Paint.
- Switch among open programs.
- Share information between different programs.
- Create a shortcut to a commonly used program.
- Run an MS-DOS–based program from an MS-DOS prompt.

You can practice the skills you learned in Part 2 by working through the steps in this Review & Practice section.

Scenario

As the coordinator of a series of "brown bag" lunch presentations for Childs Play, Inc. employees, you want to create a flyer, with an eye-catching graphic, to publicize the events.

Step 1: Create a Text Document Using WordPad

In this step, you open a document and format the text for the brown bag lunch presentation flyer.

Edit a document

1   Use the Start button to start WordPad.

2   On the toolbar, click Open. Open the Windows NT Practice folder. Open the Brown Bag Presentations document.

3   Change the presentation topic "Vacation Tips" to "Vacation Planning Tips."

4   In the presentation topic "So You're Interested in Skin Diving and Scuba Diving?" delete the words "Skin Diving and."

5   Change the presentation topic "Avoiding Strain at Work" to "Avoiding Strain at Your Computer."

6   Save your changes.

Format a document

1   Select all the text in the document.

2   Center all the text. (Hint: Use the Center button on the format bar.)

3   Change the font of all the text in the document to Arial.

4   Change "Announcing" to 18-point bold type.

5   Change "Topics for April" to 14-point bold type.

6   Change the line that begins with "Brown Bag Presentations" to italic type.

7   Save your changes.

For more information on	See
Using WordPad	Lesson 4

Step 2:   *Create a Drawing Using Paint*

In this step, you design the graphic that you will use to represent and help publicize the brown bag lunch presentations.

Create a new graphic

1   Use the Start button to start Paint.

2   In the Paint window, use the Rectangle, Ellipse, and Line tools to create the following shapes.

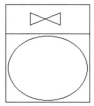

3 Use the Text tool to type **Brown Bag Lunch Presentations** in the graphic. Change the font to 16-point bold italic type.

4 Use the Airbrush tool to create a brush effect.

Your graphic should look similar to the following illustration.

5 Save the document in the Windows NT Practice folder, and name it **Brown Bag Logo**

Select, copy, and paste shapes

1 Use the Select tool to select and copy the line design.

2 Paste the line design.

3 Move the pasted line design beneath the rectangle of the graphic.

Your graphic should look similar to the following illustration.

4 Save your changes.

Add color to the graphic

1 Use the Fill With Color tool to fill areas of the graphic with colors.

Your graphic should look similar to the following illustration.

2 Save your changes.

For more information on	See
Using Paint	Lesson 5

Step 3: Share Information Between Programs

You're now ready to put the flyer together. In this step, you copy the Paint graphic into the WordPad flyer.

1 Select and copy the entire Paint graphic.

2 Switch to the WordPad document.

3 Paste the graphic at the very top of the document.

4 Save the document.

5 Print the document.

6 Close all open windows.

For more information on	See
Sharing information between different programs	Lesson 6

Step 4: Create a Shortcut to Paint

You are using Paint daily and want to be able to access it more quickly. In this step, you find the Paint program file on your hard disk, and then create a shortcut to it on your Desktop.

1 Find the Paint program file on your hard disk (C:). (Hint: Use the Find command to look for a program called "pbrush.")

2 Use your mouse to create a shortcut from the Paint program file in the Winnt\system32 folder to your Desktop.

3 Use the shortcut to start Paint.

4 Close all open windows.

For more information on	See
Finding and using Windows NT-based programs	Lesson 6

Step 5: *Use an MS-DOS–Based Program*

In this step, you open an MS-DOS window, and start the Edit program so that you can type the letter you want to send to the presenters of your Brown Bag series.

1 Open an MS-DOS window.

2 Start the MS-DOS text editor named Edit. (Hint: Type **edit** at the MS-DOS prompt.) Press ESC to close the dialog box which appears in the center of the Edit window.

3 Type the following text, pressing ENTER wherever necessary to move to the next line.

> **Attached is our schedule for the Brown Bag Lunch Presentations. Please call me if you need any special equipment for your presentation. Thank you!**

4 Exit from the Edit program without saving the file.

5 Exit from the MS-DOS command window.

For more information on	See
Using MS-DOS–based programs	Lesson 6 *and* Appendix C

Finish the Review & Practice

In the following steps, you will return your computer to the settings it had when you started this Review & Practice.

1 Close all open windows.

2 If any window is minimized, use the right mouse button to click the window's taskbar button, and then click Close.

3 Delete the Shortcut To Paint from the Desktop. Click it, press DELETE, and then click Yes or drag it to Recycle Bin.

You are now ready to start the next lesson, or you can work on your own.

4 If you are finished using Windows NT for now, on the Start menu, click Shut Down, and then click Yes.

Sharing, Organizing, and Backing Up Information

Sharing Information with Other People on Your Network

Estimated time
30 min.

In this lesson you will learn how to:

- Find out what computers and resources are available on your network.
- Share information with others on your network.
- Send electronic messages using Microsoft Exchange.

Business is often conducted in teams or workgroups. Members of these teams might share information through face-to-face meetings or via telephone. They might also exchange memos, reports, and other documents through faxes or e-mail messages. Additionally, there is often a common area such as a library or media resource center where information for general use is available. Windows NT provides the environment and the tools you need to easily communicate, share information and work with members of your team on a daily basis.

In this lesson, you'll learn how you can use your organization's network to exchange information such as files and e-mail. You'll also learn how to find information that is stored on another computer on your network.

Working with Computers on a Network

Many companies connect all their computers together on a *network* so that co-workers can share information. A network is a system of multiple computers that uses special connectivity programs, called *networking programs*, to share resources among the connected computers. For example, instead of connecting each computer to its own printer, five or ten computers can share one printer on a network. Software and other files that everyone on the network uses can be stored on a central computer, called a *server* (or *file server*), and easily accessed. Document folders containing files that need to be shared among work teams can be accessed through the network. Users on the network can also send *electronic mail*, or *e-mail*, to each other to communicate more efficiently.

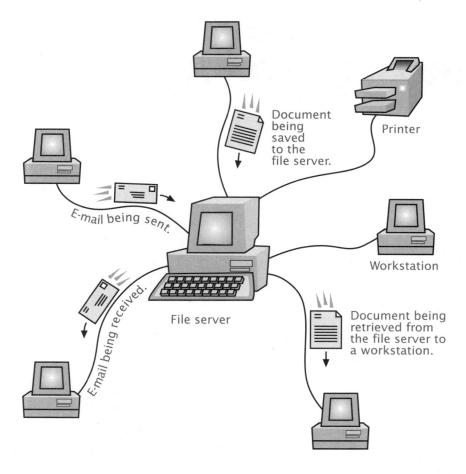

Document being saved to the file server.

Printer

E-mail being sent.

Workstation

E-mail being received.

File server

Document being retrieved from the file server to a workstation.

IMPORTANT In order to perform the exercises in this section, your computer needs to be part of a network. Your computer must include a network interface card and be physically cabled to other computers on the network. If you need to install and set up network and file sharing services, double-click the Network icon in Control Panel, and use the Network dialog box. For more information about your organization's network, contact your system administrator.

Finding Out What Computers and Resources Are Available On Your Network

Just as My Computer displays the folders and files you have stored on your computer, Network Neighborhood displays the outside resources that are available in the wider computing community of your network. Such resources can include other computers, drives, folders, files, and printers. You can use Network Neighborhood to browse through, open, explore, and use the resources available throughout your network.

Network Neighborhood works in a similar manner as My Computer—the main difference is that it displays the contents of multiple computers in a window, rather than just the contents of a single computer.

You can establish connections with other computers on your network, and then browse through the *shared resources* on those computers—folders and files that users on the network have identified as being available to others.

Browse through Network Neighborhood

Suppose you want to find out what other computers and network resources are available to you. In this exercise, you use Network Neighborhood to browse through your network.

1 Double-click the Network Neighborhood icon.

The Network Neighborhood window appears, showing the computers to which you have access on your network, as well as the Entire Network icon. Your screen might look similar to the following illustration.

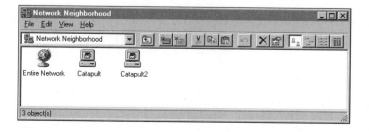

2 Double-click the Entire Network icon.

The Entire Network window appears. Your screen might look similar to the following illustration.

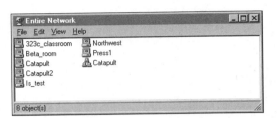

3 If you find a computer to which you want to connect, double-click its icon.

The contents of the computer that are available to you appear in a window.

4 Double-click a folder that you want to open.

The contents of the folder appear in another window.

5 Repeat this procedure to browse through as many folders as you want.

6 Close all open windows.

Using Information from Network Computers

To access information on another computer which the user or system administrator has already made accessible to you, you designate a drive on that computer as a *virtual* drive, with a unique designation, such as K: or W:. A virtual drive acts like a real disk drive on your machine, but is in fact a network connection, rather than an actual physical drive. This one-to-one correspondence between your virtual drives and computers on the network is called *mapping*. Using Windows NT Explorer, My Computer, or Network Neighborhood, you can map a virtual drive on your computer to any disk drive (or folder on a disk drive) that has been designated as shared. Once you are connected to a network disk drive, you can see the folders, files, and other resources available.

Mapping a network drive is useful when you already know the name of the network computer to which you want to connect. It establishes the connection immediately and allows you to see the folders and files on the other computer, rather than having to browse through many computers that might be available on your network. Mapping a network drive is also useful when you connect to the same network computer often because it allows you to keep the connection available until you decide to disconnect it.

When you connect to a network drive, you indicate the drive letter you want to use. The letter A, and sometimes B, is typically reserved for your floppy disk drives. The letter C is usually reserved for your hard disk. Other drive letters might be used if you have an additional hard disk, a CD-ROM drive, or a tape drive installed on your computer, or if other network drive designations have already been established.

You can either map a drive letter to a specific folder on a computer, or to an entire computer so you can have access to all the shared folders stored on that computer.

You can map the network drives you use regularly to virtual drives on your computer, and have your computer establish these connections automatically each time you log on.

When you connect to a network drive, you also specify the *path*—the name and location of the computer and folder to which you want to connect. The path is entered in the following format: *computername**foldername*. For example, if the name of the computer is Accounts, and the folder you want to connect to is named Midwest, the path is \\Accounts\Midwest. In order to map to a network location, you will need to know the full path to the computer and folder you want to map to. If you don't know the exact name of the computer or folder, you can browse through Network Neighborhood to find the path.

⌐ **WARNING** If you are not sure about the actions you're taking on the network with the exercises in this section, contact your system administrator.

Map a network drive

In this exercise, you map a network drive so that you can connect to a specific computer, and quickly access and use its resources.

1 Open Windows NT Explorer.

2 Be sure that the toolbar appears in the window. If the toolbar is not showing, on the View menu, click Toolbar.

Map Network
Drive

3 On the toolbar, click the Map Network Drive button.

The Map Network Drive dialog box appears.

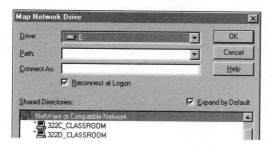

If drive W is already being used by another device or network connection, choose another available drive letter.

4 In the Drive list box, type **W** or select "W" from the drop-down list of available drives.

The letter indicates the drive designation you want to use for the computer and folder to which you're mapping.

You can also select the path to the computer in the Paths box, if you have previously been connected to it.

5   In the Path box, type the path to the computer to which you want to map the network drive using the *computername**foldername* format, where "computer name" and "folder name" are the names of a computer and folder on your network.

If you want your computer to automatically connect to this computer the next time you log on, select the Reconnect At Logon check box.

6   Click OK. If a password is required for you to map to this computer and folder, the Password dialog box appears. Type the password, and then click OK.

A new network drive icon appears in the Exploring window.

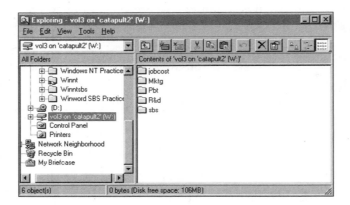

When you map to a shared folder, a window opens to display its contents.

 TIP   You don't have to map a network drive in order to use a network resource. You can open any network resource using the Run command on the Start menu. In the Run dialog box, type the path in the *computername**foldername* format, and then click OK. The Run command is a convenient way to temporarily access a network computer when you know its path, but don't plan on using it very often.

View information on another computer

Now that your network drive is mapped, you can look at the files stored on the drive. In this exercise, you browse through the available files stored on another computer on your network.

1   Be sure that the window displaying the contents of the network drive you
connected to in the previous exercise is open. If it is not open, double-
click its drive icon in the Exploring window.

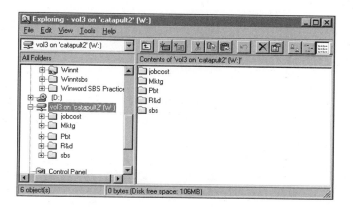

*You can tell
what program a
file is associated
with by looking
at its icon.*

2   Browse through the folders and files, and open any file that was created
using a program that you have on your computer, such as WordPad or
Paint.

You can open and view any shared file from a network computer as long
as you have the program that was used to create the file is set up on your
own computer.

3   Close all open windows.

TIP   If you want to copy a file from another computer onto your
computer, drag the file to copy it from the other computer to the
folder of your choice on your hard disk.

Disconnect a mapped drive

If you decide you no longer need a network drive, you can disconnect it as easily as you connected it. In this exercise, you disconnect a mapped network
drive.

1   Open Windows NT Explorer.

*Disconnect
Net Drive*

2   On the toolbar, click the Disconnect Net Drive button.

The Disconnect Network Drive dialog box appears.

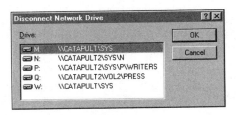

3 From the list of mapped drives, click drive W or the drive letter you selected, and then click OK. Be sure to only select the drive you want to disconnect from before clicking OK.

The drive W icon disappears from the Exploring window.

 TIP In addition to using the toolbar buttons, you can map and disconnect network drives by using the right mouse button. You can click the Network Neighborhood icon with the right mouse button, and then choose Map Network Drive or Disconnect Net Drive on the shortcut menu.

Making Information Available on the Network

You can make information you have on your computer available to others on your network. If you have the appropriate access permissions, you can make information available on the network by copying to a server, another individual's computer, or any other network computer.

If your network uses a server (a centralized computer to which the other computers in the network are connected), you can copy your files to the server, just as if you were copying them to another drive. After you have copied your files to the server, users on your network can access, view or edit the files. Copying files to a network server is an efficient way of sharing information because others can access the files directly from the server instead of from your computer (which might significantly slow down the performance of your computer).

If your network connects all computers to one another, rather than to a server, you can make information on your computer available to others. When you designate a shared folder on your computer, another user on your network can connect or map to your computer, and then access, view or edit the contents of the shared folder.

You can control which folders are available to other network users. Folders available to other network users are called *public folders*. Folders not available to others are called *private folders*.

You can add another level of security to your shared files by setting *passwords*. If you want to control who has access to certain folders, you can set a password for those folders. Only the individuals to whom you give the password are able to read, change, and save the files contained in the folder. You can also set a separate password for read-only access. You can even establish several combinations of privileges and passwords as necessary.

Copy a file to another computer

Suppose you work on a network computer system that uses shared resources. In this exercise, you copy a file to another computer on your network to make it available to other network users.

1   Using Windows NT Explorer, open the Windows NT Practice folder.

2   In the Windows NT Practice folder, click the History file once to select it.

3   On the Edit menu, click Copy.

4   Open any shared network drive currently connected to your computer.

If there are no shared network drives mapped to your computer, connect to one following the steps listed in the exercise titled "Map a network drive," earlier in this lesson.

5   On the Edit menu of the shared network drive window, click Paste.

The History file is copied to the shared network drive, unless that drive is set up to deny you privileges to write to it.

6   Close all open windows.

 WARNING   Certain networks do not handle filenames that are longer than eight characters. If you copy a file with a long filename across a network that has a eight-character limit, the long filename will be truncated. Because this can make different files appear to have the same name, be careful not to accidentally overwrite an important file this way.

Designate a folder as a shared resource

Suppose you want to identify one of your folders for public use. This offers an alternative to copying your folders and files to another computer, and can accommodate the type of network you might have. When you identify a folder as a shared resource, the folder stays on your computer, but other users can access it. In this exercise, you set a folder on your computer as a shared resource.

1   Using Windows NT Explorer, open your hard disk (C:).

2   Click the Windows NT Practice folder to select it.

3   On the File menu, click Properties.

The Windows NT Practice Properties dialog box appears. Click the Sharing tab to make it active.

4   Click the Shared As option button.

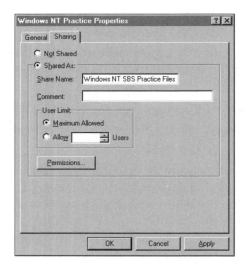

5   In the Comment box, type **Windows NT Practice Files**, and then click OK. Click Yes to close the Sharing dialog box.

The folder icon changes to indicate that the folder is now a shared resource.

6   Close all open windows.

Sending Information Using Microsoft Exchange

You can think of Microsoft Exchange as your computer's "post office." Microsoft Exchange can manage all of your telecommunication business. It allows you to send and receive messages, whether they are electronic mail messages, fax messages, online service messages, or files. Microsoft Exchange also stores copies of your outgoing messages for future reference, and alerts you when you have unread messages.

Send a mail message

In this exercise, you send an e-mail message using Microsoft Exchange.

 IMPORTANT   To perform this exercise, you need to be set up to exchange mail with other users, either on a network or through modem connections. If you are not set up to exchange mail with other users, you can skip this exercise.

If you see the Microsoft Exchange Setup Wizard, it means you still need to specify your communication choices on your computer. Follow the instructions to complete your Microsoft Exchange profile.

1 On your Desktop, double-click the Inbox icon.

The Microsoft Exchange window appears. Your screen should look similar to the following illustration.

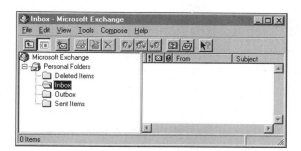

2 On the Compose menu, click New Message.

The New Message window appears.

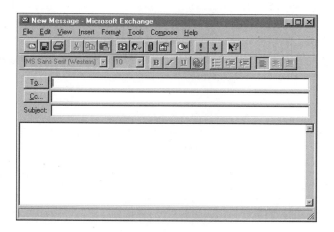

If you do not know your e-mail username, check with your system administrator.

3 In the To box, type your e-mail username.

This will cause the message to be sent back to you, just for practice.

4 In the Subject box, type **Testing Microsoft Exchange**

5 In the message area, type the following message:

I am testing Microsoft Exchange in Windows NT.

Send

6 On the toolbar, click the Send button.

The message is sent to you after a few moments and a copy is saved in your Sent Items folder.

141

Send an attachment

Imagine you need one of your colleagues to review a file you worked on online. The easiest way to pass the file on is to attach it to an e-mail message. In this exercise, you send an attachment.

1   On the Compose menu, click New Message.

2   In the To box, type your e-mail username.

This will cause the message to be sent back to you, just for practice.

3   In the Subject box, type **Testing Sending an Attachment**

4   In the message area, type the following message:

Now I'm testing sending an attachment.

Insert File

5   On the toolbar, click the Insert File button.

Locate the Windows NT Practice folder, and then click the History document.

6   Click OK.

Microsoft Exchange displays an icon of the History document in the body of the message.

Send

7   On the toolbar, click the Send button.

The message is sent to you with the file attachment, and a copy is saved in your Sent Items folder.

Save an attachment

Suppose you just received an e-mail message that contains a file you need to review online. In this exercise, you save an attachment on your hard disk.

1   Open the mail message that contains the attachment you want to save.

2   Click the attachment to select it.

3   On the File menu, click Save As.

4   Select the folder where you want to save the attachment on your hard disk (C:), and then click OK.

One Step Further: Protect a Shared Folder So That Others Can Read Information But Not Change It

You can define different levels of access to your folders: no access, read, change, or full control. If you designate your folder with read access, network users will only be able to open and read the files; they will not be able to change its contents. If your folder has full control access, other users will be able to open and read as well as edit its files.

1   Using Windows NT Explorer, open the hard disk (C:).

2   Click the Windows NT Practice folder to select it.

3   On the File menu, click Properties.

The Windows NT Practice Properties dialog box appears.

4   Click the Sharing tab.

5   Click the Permissions button.

6   In the Type Of Access drop-down list box, select Read.

This will allow other users to view but not modify the contents of the folder.

7   Click OK.

8   Click OK to close the Properties dialog box.

9   Close all open windows.

Finish the lesson

In the following steps, you will return your computer to the settings it had when you started this lesson. You will also close any open windows.

1   Using Windows NT Explorer, open the shared network drive into which you copied the History file. Delete the History file by dragging it from its network location to Recycle Bin.

 WARNING   Be sure to delete only the History file from the network drive. If you have any doubts about the file you should delete, contact your system administrator.

---

2   Using Windows NT Explorer, open the hard disk (C:), and then click the Windows NT Practice folder. On the File menu, click Properties. In the Properties dialog box, click the Sharing tab, click the Not Shared option button, and then click OK.

The icon changes, to indicate that the file is no longer shared.

![X] *Close*

3   Close all open windows by clicking the Close button in the upper-right corner of each window.

4   If any window is minimized, use the right mouse button to click the window's taskbar button, and then click Close.

You are now ready to start the next lesson, or you can work on your own.

5   If you are finished using Windows NT for now, on the Start menu, click Shut Down, and then click Yes.

Lesson Summary

To	Do this	Button
Open Windows NT Explorer	On the Start menu, point to Programs, and then click Windows NT Explorer.	
Map a network drive	On the Windows NT Explorer toolbar, click the Map Network Drive button. In the Drive box, type the drive letter, and then type or select the path to the computer and folder on the network. Click OK.	
Open and browse through a mapped network drive	In the Exploring window, double-click the network drive's icon. The shared folders and files on that drive appear.	
Open and browse through Network Neighborhood	Double-click the Network Neighborhood icon. Double-click Entire Network or any computer icons that appear.	
Disconnect a mapped drive	In the Exploring window, click the network drive icon. On the toolbar, click the Disconnect Net Drive button.	
Set a folder or file on your computer as a shared resource for the network	In the Exploring window, click the folder or file you want to share. On the File menu, click Properties. Click the Sharing tab, and then click Shared As. Enter additional information in the Comment box, and then click OK.	
Send a mail message using Microsoft Exchange	Double-click the Inbox icon. On the Compose menu, click New Message. Fill in the message, and then click Send.	

For online information about	From the Help Topics dialog box, click Index, and then type
Mapping and disconnecting a network drive	**mapping, drive letters**
Browsing through a network drive	**networks, finding files or folders on**
Sharing drives, folders, or files on the network	**sharing**
Sending mail messages using Microsoft Exchange	**mail**

Finding and Organizing Files and Folders

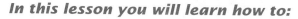

In this lesson you will learn how to:

- Find document files and program files stored on your own computer or on the network.
- Create folders and move files.
- Rename and copy your files and folders.
- Delete unwanted files and folders.
- Browse through your computer's filing system.

Estimated time
30 min.

Manually searching for a program file or a document file can be not only difficult but also time consuming. However, with Microsoft Windows NT, you can easily find files located on your computer or the network using the Find command. It searches for all the files that match the criteria you specify, and then generates a list.

For example, you can search for all the files that have the word "Marketing" in their name or that contain the word "Marketing" in the file. You can also search for a particular type of file such as program files or picture files, or even combine different search criteria to narrow your search down.

In this lesson, you'll learn how to locate different types of files on your computer or on the network, as well as organize your hard disk by creating folders, moving files, renaming files, and deleting unneeded items.

Finding Files

Up to this point, you've been searching for your files by browsing through My Computer or Windows NT Explorer. When you know in which folder a file is located, browsing is probably the most convenient way to find it. But, what do you do if you know part of the filename, but don't have any idea where it might be on the hard disk?

The Find command offers a versatile way to search your computer for files. In the following exercises, you'll use the Find command to locate files using three different search criteria.

Find files by name

Suppose you have created a document file, but you don't remember the folder in which you saved it. In this exercise, you find and open a document file using the Find command.

1 If your computer isn't already on, turn it on now. If necessary, press CTRL+ALT+DELETE to log on. Type your password if you're using one, and then press ENTER. If you see the Welcome dialog box, click the Close button.

2 Click Start. On the Start menu, point to Find.

3 On the Find menu, click Files Or Folders.

The Find dialog box appears.

4 Be sure that the Name & Location tab is active and that the Include Subfolders check box is selected.

The Named list box maintains a list of your previous search terms.

5 In the Named box, type **logo**, and then click the Find Now button.

All files throughout your hard disk that have "logo" as part of their filenames are listed in the bottom half of the dialog box. Also listed are the folders in which the files are stored, the file sizes in kilobytes (KB), and the file types.

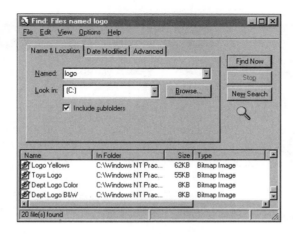

6 In the resulting list of files, scroll to Dept Logo Color, and then double-click it.

The Paint program starts, and then the Dept Logo Color file appears in the Paint window.

7 Close the Paint window.

Find files by file type

You can search for a file by *file type* if you have forgotten its exact name or location. The file type is the file category, such as bitmap image file, application (program) file, folder, shortcut, or WordPad document. In this exercise, you search for program and bitmap image files.

1 With the Find dialog box still open, click the New Search button, and then click OK.

This clears all the previous search criteria in all three tabs.

2 Click the Advanced tab to make it active.

3 On the Of Type list box, click the down arrow.

A list of file types appears.

4 Click Application, and then click the Find Now button.

Windows NT searches throughout the disk specified in the Look In box of the Name & Location tab, and lists all the program files found on your hard disk.

5 In the search list, scroll to, and then double-click Charmap, which is the program file for the Character Map accessory.

The Character Map starts. Your screen should look similar to the following illustration.

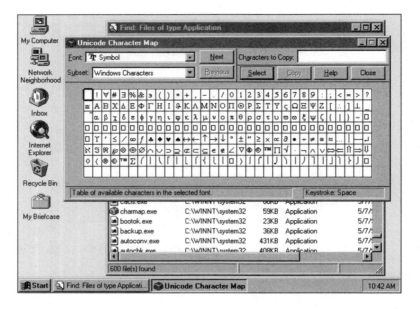

6 On the taskbar, click the Find button.

The Find dialog box appears again.

7 Open the Of Type list box again, click Bitmap Image, and then click the Find Now button.

All bitmap image files on your hard disk, such as the logo files located in the Windows NT Practice folder, are listed.

Find files by the date they were last modified

Suppose you have set up a new program in the last week, but you have not yet added a shortcut to it on the Programs menu or the Desktop, and you don't remember where the program is. In this exercise, you find the program file, and then start the program.

New files will also be found when you execute a search using the Date Modified tab.

1 With the Find dialog box still open, click the New Search button, and then click OK.

2 Click the Date Modified tab to make it active.

3 Click the Between option button, and then type the date from one week ago.

4 Press TAB, and then type the current date.

5 Click the Find Now button.

Windows NT displays all the documents that were modified within the date range you specified.

6 Close all open windows.

Organizing Your Files

Depending on the nature of your work and the way you like to organize it, your filing scheme can take different forms. You might have a separate folder for each type of project, for example, letters, status reports, and budget forecasts. If you work with different clients, you might prefer to designate a separate folder for each client. If several individuals use one computer, as in a family or small business setting, you might want to set up a separate folder for each user. In any case, Windows NT offers the tools you need to efficiently manage your files by allowing you to easily create folders and move files. By adopting and adhering to a particular organizational scheme, you can keep your files in logical order for quick and easy access.

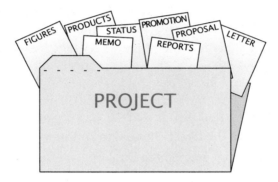

If you're having trouble finding your files in a folder...

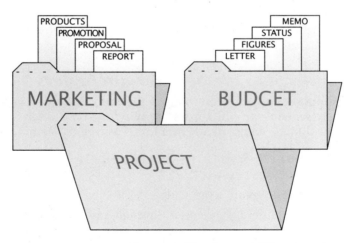

...you can organize your files into additional subfolders within the original folder.

151

Creating Folders and Moving Files

You can create folders with descriptive names by taking advantage of the long filename capabilities of Windows NT, and then move the files in the most appropriate folders.

Create folders

Suppose that after browsing through your computer filing system, you think of a more efficient way to organize your files. You decide to group related files by tables, employee information, and product line information. In this exercise, you create these three folders and setup your new file organization scheme.

1 Double-click the My Computer icon to open it. Double-click on the hard disk (C:) icon, and then the Windows NT Practice folder icon.

   The Windows NT Practice folder window opens.

2 On the File menu of the Windows NT Practice window, point to New, and then click Folder.

   A new folder, named New Folder, appears at the bottom of the window. The name is selected, so you can easily replace it by typing over.

3 Type **Tables**, and then press ENTER.

   The name of the folder changes to Tables.

4 Click an empty area on the Desktop.

5 Repeat steps 2 and 3 to create an Employee Information folder and a Product Line folder.

6 On the View menu, point to Arrange Icons, and then click By Name.

   This rearranges all of your icons, so that the folders appear in alphabetical order followed by files listed in alphabetical order.

Move files into the appropriate folders

Now, suppose that you want to move files into the folders you just created. In this exercise, you move files from the Windows NT Practice folder into the appropriate folders, using menu commands as well as the mouse.

1 With the Windows NT Practice folder still open, click the Personnel Letter file icon once to select it.

You can also press CTRL+X to cut the selected file.

2 On the Edit menu, click Cut.

   The Personnel Letter icon is dimmed, indicating that it's in the middle of an operation.

3 Double-click the new Employee Information folder to open it.

   The Employee Information window appears.

You can also press CTRL+V to paste the selected file.

4 On the Edit menu of the Employee Information window, click Paste.

The Personnel Letter file appears in the Employee Information folder and disappears from the Windows NT Practice folder.

5 On the taskbar, click Windows NT Practice.

The Windows NT Practice folder appears.

6 In the Windows NT Practice window, drag the 1997 Product Line icon to the Tables folder until the Tables folder changes color, and then release the mouse button.

1997 Product Line moves to the Tables folder and is no longer listed in the Windows NT Practice folder.

7 Double-click the Tables folder icon.

The Tables window appears, along with the moved file.

You can use these procedures to move a folder into another folder.

8 Either use the Cut and Paste commands on the Edit menu, or drag with the mouse to move the following files into the indicated folders.

Move this file	To this folder
Investment Portfolio	Employee Information
Employee Table	Tables
Product IDs	Tables
Employee Handbook	Employee Information
1997 Product Line	Product Line
Product Descriptions	Product Line

9 Close all open windows.

Renaming and Copying Files and Folders

You can rename your files to make the filenames more descriptive or to take advantage of the long filename capabilities of Windows NT. You can also copy files to other folders or to the Desktop.

Rename files and folders

Suppose you want to rename several files to make the filenames consistent with the new file naming conventions that were recently developed in your company. In this exercise, you rename two files using two different methods.

1 On the Start menu, point to Programs, and then click Windows NT Explorer.

2 Double-click the hard disk (C:) icon.

3 Double-click the Windows NT Practice folder.

4 In the contents list, click the Company Background file once to select it.

5 On the File menu, click Rename.

The filename is highlighted and an insertion point appears at the end of the filename.

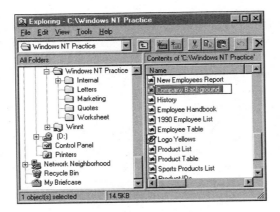

6 Type **Childs Play History**, and then press ENTER.

7 Use the right mouse button to click the Brown Bag WordPad file.

The file is selected, and a shortcut menu appears.

You can also use these procedures to rename a folder.

8 On the shortcut menu, click Rename.

An insertion point appears at the end of the selected filename.

9 Type **Brown Bag Lunch**, and then press ENTER.

The filename changes.

 TIP You can also rename files with My Computer. In the My Computer window, select the file you want to rename, and then, on the File menu, click Rename.

Copy files to another folder

Suppose you have files in one folder, and you want to put copies of these files in another folder. In this exercise, you copy files between folders.

1 With the Windows NT Practice folder still open, click the Sports Products List file icon in the contents list of the Exploring window to select it.

You can also press CTRL+C to copy a file.

2 On the Edit menu, click Copy.

The Sports Products List file is copied to the computer's memory, but nothing changes on the screen.

You can also press CTRL+V to paste a file.

3 Double-click the Marketing folder.

4 On the Edit menu of the active window, click Paste.

A copy of the Sports Products List file appears in the Marketing folder.

5 In the folders list, double-click the Windows NT Practice folder.

All of the folders and files in the Windows NT Practice folder appear in the contents list of the Exploring window.

If your screen looks different from this illustration, see Appendix B, "Matching the Exercises."

6 In the contents list, drag Chklist.ms to the Letters folder until the folder icon changes color.

While you're dragging, your mouse pointer displays a plus sign to indicate that you are copying rather than moving.

First, select the file you want to copy...

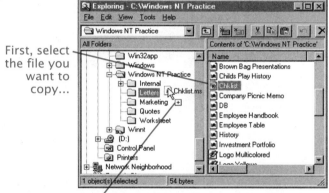

...then, hold down CTRL and drag the file to the folder icon until it changes color.

7 Double-click the Letters folder.

All of the files contained in the Letters folder are displayed in the contents list, including Chklist.ms.

TIP You can also copy and paste files with My Computer. In the My Computer window, click the file you want to copy, and then, on the Edit menu, click Copy. Open the folder where you want to copy the file, and then on the Edit menu, click Paste.

Deleting Files and Folders

Another aspect of organizing your files and folders is cleanup. You can delete backup or temporary files as well as old files you don't use anymore to free up space on your hard disk.

Any deleted files or folders are placed in Recycle Bin. If you change your mind before you empty Recycle Bin, you can "recycle" an item and reuse it by retrieving it from Recycle Bin.

Delete files

Let's say you have multiple versions of the same file, and don't need them anymore. In this exercise, you delete files and an entire folder using Recycle Bin.

1 On the taskbar, click Windows NT Practice.

The Windows NT Practice window becomes active.

2 Drag the 1990 Employee List to the Recycle Bin icon on your Desktop.

The 1990 Employee List file no longer appears in the Windows NT Practice window. You have just moved it to Recycle Bin, a holding area for files and folders you no longer need.

3 In the Windows NT Practice window, use the right mouse button to click the Retirement Planning Backup file.

A shortcut menu appears.

You can also delete a file by selecting it and pressing DELETE.

4 On the shortcut menu, click Delete.

The Confirm File Delete dialog box appears.

5 Click Yes.

The Retirement Planning Backup file disappears from the Windows NT Practice window and is placed in Recycle Bin.

You can follow this procedure to delete files and folders from Windows NT Explorer.

6 From the Windows NT Practice window, drag the Worksheet folder to the Recycle Bin icon.

The Worksheet folder is deleted. Deleted items stay in Recycle Bin until you explicitly empty it. If you accidentally delete a file, you might be able to recover it from Recycle Bin, provided you haven't already emptied it.

Recover deleted files from Recycle Bin

Suppose you changed your mind about a file or folder you have deleted. If you have not yet emptied Recycle Bin, you can retrieve and re-use any item stored there. In this exercise, you recover a deleted file from Recycle Bin.

1 Double-click the Recycle Bin icon.

The Recycle Bin window appears, listing all the files, folders, and other files deleted since the last time Recycle Bin was emptied.

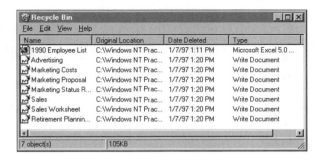

2   From the Recycle Bin window, drag 1990 Employee List back to the Windows NT Practice folder.

The 1990 Employee List file appears in the folder again, and you can use it as if it had never been deleted.

3   Close the Recycle Bin window.

TIP   Another way to recover files from Recycle Bin is to click the item, and then, on the Recycle Bin File menu, click Restore. The file returns to its original folder, even if the folder is not currently open.

Empty Recycle Bin

Items in Recycle Bin take up space on your hard disk. If you're deleting files and folders to make more room on your hard disk, you should empty Recycle Bin to actually free up some space. In this exercise, you first delete selected files from Recycle Bin, and then empty it to remove all the remaining items.

1   Double-click the Recycle Bin icon.

Recycle Bin opens, displaying a list of all items deleted since the last time it was emptied. The status bar at the bottom of the Recycle Bin window indicates the number of objects in Recycle Bin, and how much disk space they occupy.

You can select multiple adjacent items by holding down SHIFT, clicking the first item, and then clicking the last item in the series.

2   Hold down CTRL and click nonadjacent items in the list, if there are any.

By holding down CTRL, you can select several nonadjacent items at one time in any list.

157

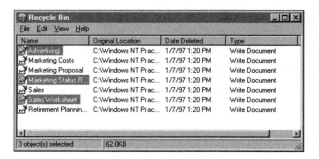

3 On the File menu, click Delete.

The Confirm Multiple File Delete dialog box appears.

To empty Recycle Bin without opening it, use the right mouse button to click Recycle Bin, and then click Empty Recycle Bin.

4 Click Yes to delete the three items from Recycle Bin and from your hard disk.

5 On the File menu, click Empty Recycle Bin.

6 In the Confirm Multiple File Delete dialog box, click Yes.

All the contents of Recycle Bin are removed from your hard disk.

7 Close all open windows.

Browsing Through Your Files

You can browse through your filing system using either My Computer or the Windows NT Explorer.

Browse through your filing system using Windows NT Explorer

In this exercise, you browse through your computer system files using Windows NT Explorer.

1 Click Start. On the Start menu, point to Programs, and then click Windows NT Explorer.

The Exploring window appears.

If the icons in your window look different from those illustrated here, on the View menu, click List to change the view.

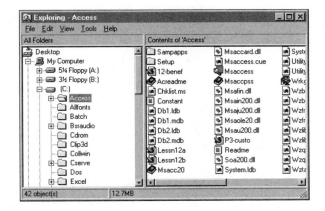

2 In the folders list, click the hard disk (C:).

The contents list displays the names of the files and folders stored on your hard disk.

3 In the folders list, double-click the Windows NT Practice folder.

The folders list displays all the folders stored in the Windows NT Practice folder. The folders are also displayed in the contents list along with the files stored in the Windows NT Practice folder.

4 In the folders list, click the Marketing folder.

The contents list displays all the files stored in the Marketing folder.

5 On the View menu, click Large Icons.

The folders and files in the contents list are now represented by large icons.

6 Display the toolbar, if necessary, by clicking Toolbar on the View menu.

The toolbar appears on the Exploring window. Make the window wider, if necessary, to view all the buttons on the toolbar.

Details

7 On the toolbar, click the Details button.

You might have to resize the window to view the entire toolbar. The display of folders and files in the contents list changes to show a list of the files with small icons, along with detailed information about each file.

One Step Further: Find a File by Its Contents

You can narrow the search criteria for a file by adding a *keyword* to the search specifications. When you use keywords, Windows NT searches for files that contain the specified word as part of the file contents. For example, you can search for any file containing the words "customer representative" by using the Advanced tab in the Find dialog box.

Find a file by its contents

Suppose you're looking for the memo and map you created for the company picnic. In this exercise, you search for these files using a keyword.

1 On the Start menu, point to Find, and then click Files and Folders.

The Find dialog box appears.

2 Click the Advanced tab.

3 On the Of Type list box, click the down arrow.

A list of file types appears.

4 Click WordPad Document.

5 In the Containing Text box, type **picnic**, and then click the Find Now button.

Windows NT searches throughout your computer system, and then lists all the WordPad files that contain the word "picnic."

Finish the lesson

Close

1 Close all open windows by clicking the Close button in the upper-right corner of each window.

2 If any window is minimized, use the right mouse button to click the window's taskbar button, and then click Close.

You are now ready to start the next lesson, or you can work on your own.

3 If you are finished using Windows NT for now, on the Start menu, click Shut Down, and then click Yes.

Lesson Summary

To	Do this
Find a program file	Click Start, point to Find, and then click Files Or Folders. On the Name & Location tab, type all or part of the name of the program. Click the Advanced tab. In the Of Type box, click Application, and then click Find Now.

To	Do this
Find a document file	Click Start, point to Find, and then click Files Or Folders. On the Name & Location tab, type all or part of the filename in the Name box, and then click Find Now.
Browse through your computer filing system using My Computer	Double-click the My Computer icon. Double-click any drives and folders you want to browse.
Browse through your computer filing system using Windows NT Explorer	Click Start, point to Programs, and then click Windows NT Explorer. In the folders list, click the drive and folders you want to browse. In the contents list, view the files stored on the drive or folder selected in the folders list.
Create a new folder	Open the drive or folder in which you want the new folder to be stored. On the File menu, point to New, and then click Folder. Type a name for the new folder, and then press ENTER.
Move a file to another folder	Drag the file to the folder in which you want to move it.
Rename a file or folder	Use the right mouse button to click the file you want to rename. On the shortcut menu, click Rename. Type the new name, and then press ENTER.
Copy a file to another folder	Hold down CTRL and drag the file you want to copy to a new location.
Delete a file	Drag the file to the Recycle Bin.
Recover a deleted file	Open Recycle Bin, and then drag the file you want to recover to the appropriate folder or drive, or to the Desktop.
Empty Recycle Bin	Open Recycle Bin, and then, on the File menu, click Empty Recycle Bin.

For online information about	From the Help Topics dialog box, click Index, and then type
Finding files	**Find command, using**
Browsing using My Computer or Windows NT Explorer	**browsing, through folders on your computer**
Creating and using folders	**folders**
Moving files and folders	**moving, files or folders**
Copying files and folders	**copying, files or folders**
Deleting files and folders	**deleting, files or folders**
Using Recycle Bin	**Recycle Bin**

Backing Up Your Important Information

Estimated time

25 min.

In this lesson you will learn how to:

- Format new floppy disks to prepare them for use in your computer.
- Back up files to a floppy disk, a network, and a tape drive.
- Restore files from a tape drive.

Although your hard disk is probably your primary storage device, you might use additional storage devices to back up your work. Periodic backups offer an invaluable protection in case your hard disk malfunctions, and they also preserve a recent copy of your work in case you accidentally delete an important file from your hard disk. Finally, if file backups are stored in another location, they provide security in case of fire or theft. For optimal protection, establish a daily routine to back up your important files, and if security is an issue, find out if the backup floppy disks or tapes could be stored in a locked cabinet or in another location away from your office.

There are several storage devices you can use to back up important files, including floppy disks, network computers or folders, or tapes. The storage device you choose depends on the information you want to back up and the backup devices available in your organization. In general, you will back up only your *data files*. Data files are the files, such as letters, drawings, or spreadsheets, that you create or modify using a program such as WordPad, Paint, Microsoft Word, or Microsoft Excel. Unless you're using a tape drive to back up your entire hard disk, it is unnecessary to back up the program files themselves, such as the Word or Excel program, since you can reinstall a program from its original floppy disk or CD-ROM.

To back up a single file that is not very large, you can choose to use a floppy disk. This method is convenient if you want to take the file with you to edit it on another computer, for example. When you back up a file to a floppy disk, the entire file must fit on one floppy disk. For this reason, using a floppy disk is not always possible. It can also be time-consuming because of the slower speed at which your computer copies the files to a floppy disk, and the amount of time it takes to insert, remove, and label disks if you back up several large files onto floppy disks.

When the files you need to back up are numerous or large, or when they don't fit on a floppy disk, the most efficient method may be to back them up to a network location. Ask your system administrator if there is a specific network location that has been designated to store backups of data files in your organization.

If you have a tape drive available on your computer, you can back up a large number of files on a tape, and then store it in another location. Depending on the frequency with which you perform the backups, this method preserves a more or less recent copy of your work that you can use to restore copies of the files in case of loss, fire, or theft.

NOTE   If you have any additional or specific questions regarding the backup of your data files, ask your system administrator.

How Files and Folders Are Stored

Your data files and folders are stored on disks. There are two types of disks commonly used with personal computers: floppy disks and hard disks. You can think of your *hard disk* as being like a series of filing cabinets built into your computer system. And, floppy disks are like file boxes that you can transport.

Your hard disk is used to store your document files and your program files. Floppy disks are used to transfer files from one computer to another and to make backup copies of files stored on the hard disk.

A floppy disk is like...   ...a file box.

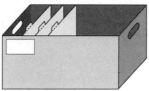

It holds a limited amount of information, but it can easily be transported between computers.

A hard disk is like...

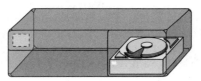
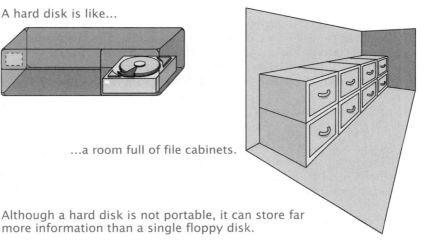

...a room full of file cabinets.

Although a hard disk is not portable, it can store far more information than a single floppy disk.

A *disk drive* is the mechanism that reads and writes information to and from a disk. Floppy disk drives are usually built into the main structure (the *system unit*) of the computer, and the floppy disks get inserted into the disk drive slots. The hard disk drive is also built into the system unit, but it is not visible from the outside.

Each disk drive has a name that is used to identify it. The first floppy disk drive is typically referred to as drive A. The second floppy disk drive is typically referred to as drive B. The hard disk is typically referred to as drive C. These names can be changed when the computer system is configured. You can also define any number of additional drives, such as CD-ROM drives, tape drives, and network drives.

There are two physical sizes for floppy disks: 3.5-inch and 5.25-inch. There are also two densities available for each disk size: high density and double density.

Each of the four types of floppy disks can hold a different amount of information, calculated in *bytes*.

Floppy disk type	Storage capacity
5.25-inch double density (DD)	360 kilobytes
5.25-inch high density (HD)	1.2 megabytes
3.5-inch double density (DD)	720 kilobytes
3.5-inch high density (HD)	1.44 megabytes

Backing Up a File to a Floppy Disk

You can use a floppy disk to make a backup copy of a file stored on your hard disk. In order to back up a file to floppy disk, the file must be small enough to fit on a single disk. If you copy your file onto a new, blank floppy disk, you must first be sure that the disk is formatted for PC-compatible computers. Then, you can copy the file from your hard disk onto the floppy disk.

Format a new floppy disk

Floppy disks are available either preformatted or unformatted. Preformatted disks are ready to use right out of the box, while unformatted disks need to be formatted before they can be used. For the purposes of this lesson, suppose you have just bought a box of unformatted floppy disks. For the computer to be able to read a disk, the disk needs to be formatted only once. You may, however, need to reformat a disk from time to time, when you want to erase everything on the disk, or if you want to use it on a different platform (such as Macintosh). The process for reformatting a used disk is the same as for formatting a brand new, unformatted disk. In this exercise, you learn how to format a new floppy disk to prepare it for use in your computer.

 ⚠ WARNING The formatting process erases any information previously stored on a floppy disk. If you use Quick Format, the floppy disk will not be scanned for errors.

1   Place a new floppy disk (or a used one containing information you can discard) in the appropriate floppy disk drive (3.5-inch or 5.25-inch).

Be sure you know whether it is a double-density or high-density floppy disk. Most floppy disks are labeled "DD" for double density or "HD" for high density.

*You can also use
the right mouse
button to click
the drive icon,
and then, on the
shortcut menu,
click Format.*

2 Double-click the My Computer icon.

The My Computer window appears.

3 Click the icon for the drive that contains the floppy disk you want to format.

Be sure to click just once to select the icon. Double-clicking will cause Windows NT to try to read the contents of the disk.

4 On the File menu, click Format.

The Format dialog box appears.

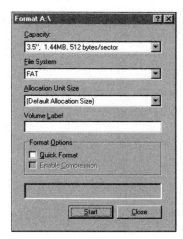

5 In the Capacity list box, verify the capacity of the floppy disk.

6 Under Format Options, select the Quick Format check box.

7 Click Start.

A warning message appears informing you that all the data on the disk will be deleted.

8 Click OK.

In the bar located at the bottom of the Format dialog box, tick marks indicate the status of the formatting process. When the floppy disk is formatted, a message indicates that the format is complete.

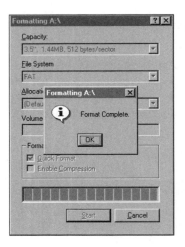

9 In the Formatting dialog box, click OK.

The Format dialog box appears again. Remove the floppy disk. If you want to format additional disks, insert a new disk, and repeat steps 5 through 8.

10 In the Format dialog box, click Close.

11 Remove the floppy disk from the drive, and write on the label "Windows NT Disk Practice."

Back up files from your hard disk to a floppy disk

Now that your floppy disk is formatted, you're ready to copy files onto it from your hard disk. You do this to make a backup of your files in case your hard disk malfunctions or to transfer files to another computer. In this exercise, you copy files, using two different methods, from the Windows NT Practice folder (on the hard disk) onto your floppy disk.

1 Insert the Windows NT Disk Practice disk you formatted in the previous exercise in the floppy disk drive.

2 Using Windows NT Explorer, open the hard disk (C:) and the Windows NT Practice folder.

3 In the Windows NT Practice folder, click Brown Bag Lunch.

4 On the File menu, point to Send To, and then click 3½ floppy.

The Brown Bag Lunch file is copied to the floppy disk.

5 On the taskbar, click My Computer, and then double-click the appropriate floppy disk drive icon, either Drive A or Drive B.

The Drive window appears, containing the icon for the Brown Bag Lunch file.

6   On the taskbar, click the Exploring–Windows NT Practice button.

The Windows NT Practice window appears.

7   Arrange the floppy drive window so that at least part of it is visible under the Windows NT Practice window.

8   From the Windows NT Practice window, drag the Brown Bag Presentations file to the floppy disk window.

Your mouse pointer takes the form of a plus sign to indicate the file is being copied to the floppy disk.

When dragging between a floppy disk and the hard disk, the item is automatically copied rather than moved. To move an item rather than copy it, hold down SHIFT while you drag.

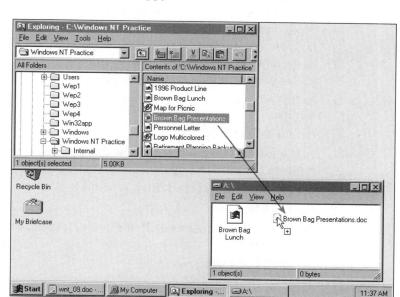

9   Close all open windows.

Backing Up Files to the Network

Another way of backing up information is to copy it to a network computer. Your organization may designate a specific network location as the place where you should back up your data files. If you are unsure where to copy files to the network for backup and what backup methods are available, ask your system administrator. Additionally, your organization might own software that gives you backup options such as automatic backups and file compression.

Back up files to a network location

In this exercise, you copy files from your computer to a network location. The network copies serve as a backup just as if you had copied the files to a floppy disk.

1   Open Windows NT Explorer.

2   On the toolbar, click the Map Network Drive button.

Map Network Drive

The Map Network Drive dialog box appears.

3   In the Drive list box, type **W** or select "W" from the list of available drives to specify the drive you want to map.

If drive W is already being used by another device or network connection, choose another drive designation.

4   In the Path box, select the path to the network computer and folder where you want to back up your files, and then click OK.

5   In the Windows NT Practice folder, click the Marketing folder once to select it.

6   On the Edit menu, click Copy.

7   In the folders list, double-click the drive letter that you used to map the network location in step 3.

For example, if you used drive W, double-click the W disk drive icon.

8   On the Edit menu, click Paste.

The Marketing folder and all of the files it contains are copied to the other computer.

9   Close all open windows.

Backing Up Files to a Tape Drive

Windows NT includes an accessory called Backup that makes it easy for you to save your important files on tape. Then, if files are accidentally deleted from your hard disk, if your hard disk fails, or if you have other computer problems, you can easily restore your files from the tape by using the Backup accessory.

> **NOTE**   If you don't have a tape drive on your computer, skip the following exercises.

Back up files to a tape drive with the Windows NT Backup tool

In this exercise, you backup files to a tape. You could back up a single file or an entire hard disk using the same technique.

1   Insert a tape in the tape drive.

2   Click Start. On the Start menu, point to Programs, point to Administrative Tools (Common), and then click Backup.

The main Backup window appears. It contains a Tapes window and a Drives window, either or both of which may be minimized.

3   If the Drives window is minimized, on the Window menu, click Drives.

4   On the Window menu, click Refresh.

The information in the Drives window is updated.

5   Double-click the disk drive that contains the files you want to back up.

6   Click the check boxes on the toolbar next to the folders or files you want to back up.

An X appears in the box to the left of each file name or disk drive that you selected.

7   Click the Backup button on the toolbar.

The Backup Information dialog box appears.

8   Note the name of the backup log in the Log File box, and then click OK.

The files you selected are backed up onto the tape.

Restoring Files from a Tape Drive

If you lose your work through an accident, such as a hard disk failure, you can use Backup to restore the last copy of the files that were saved to tape.

Restore files from a tape drive with Windows NT Backup

When some or all of your data files have been lost or deleted, you can easily restore them from the tape onto which they were backed up. Let's pretend that the files you backed up in the previous exercise got lost. In this exercise, you restore files that you have backed up on a tape.

1   Insert the tape containing the files you want to restore into the tape drive, if necessary.

2   Click Start. On the Start menu, point to Programs, point to Administrative Tools (Common), and then click Backup.

The main Backup window appears. It contains a Tapes window and a Drives window, either or both of which may be minimized.

3   If the Tapes window is minimized, on the Window menu, click Tapes.

4   In the Tapes window, load the catalog of the backup set from which you want to restore certain files. The catalog contains information about the most recent back up, including a list of the folders and files you backed up.

5   Select the names of the files you want to restore.

6   Click the check boxes next to the folders or files you want to restore.

An X appears in the box to the left of each filename you selected.

7   Click the Restore button on the toolbar.

The Restore Information dialog box appears.

8   Click OK.

The files you selected are copied onto your hard drive. You might have to click Yes To All to replace files with the same name.

9   Click OK.

One Step Further: Restoring Files from a Floppy Disk to a Hard Disk

If you have previously backed up a few important files onto a floppy disk, and then happen to lose those files from your hard disk, either from an accidental deletion, a hard disk failure, or another mishap, you can easily copy them from your floppy disk back onto your hard drive. In the following exercises, you simulate a loss of data, and then you copy the files from your backup floppy disk.

"Lose" files from the hard disk

In this exercise, you simulate the loss of important data so that you can recover the data using your backup floppy disk.

1   Using Windows NT Explorer, open the Windows NT Practice folder.

2   Drag the Brown Bag Lunch and Brown Bag Presentations files to Recycle Bin.

The files are deleted.

3   Close any open windows.

Copy files from a floppy disk to the hard disk

Now that you have "lost" your important files, you decide to use your floppy disk backup to get them back. In this exercise, you use the floppy disk backup to restore the files to their original locations on your hard disk.

1   Click Start. On the Start menu, point to Programs, and then click Windows NT Explorer.

2   Insert your floppy disk labeled "Windows NT Disk Practice" into the floppy disk drive.

3   In the folders list, double-click the appropriate floppy drive icon.

The Brown Bag Lunch and Brown Bag Presentations files appear in the contents list.

4   In the folders list, scroll until the Windows NT Practice folder is visible. If necessary, double-click the hard disk icon to make the folder visible.

5   Drag the Brown Bag Lunch and Brown Bag Presentations files from the contents list to the Windows NT Practice folder.

The files are copied from the floppy disk to the Windows NT Practice folder on your hard disk.

6   Click the Close button, and then remove the floppy disk from the drive.

Finish the lesson

Close

1   Close all open windows by clicking the Close button in the upper-right corner of each window.

2   If any window is minimized, use the right mouse button to click the window's taskbar button, and then click Close.

You are now ready to start the next lesson, or you can work on your own.

3   If you are finished using Windows NT for now, on the Start menu click Shut Down, and then click Yes.

Lesson Summary

To	Do this
Format a new floppy disk	Insert the floppy disk, and use My Computer to select the drive. On the File menu, click Format. Verify the capacity of the floppy disk, and then click Start.
Copy files and folders from the hard disk to a floppy disk or a network computer	Using My Computer or Windows NT Explorer, select the files or folders you want to copy. On the File menu, click Copy. Switch to the network computer or floppy disk where you want to copy the files, and then click Paste.

To	Do this
Copy files from the hard disk to a tape drive	Click Start, point to Programs, point to Administrative Tools (Common), and then click Backup. In the Drives window, double-click the drive that contains the files you want to back up. Click the check boxes, and then click the Backup button.
Restore files from a tape drive to the hard disk	Click Start, point to Programs, point to Administrative Tools (Common), and then click Backup. In the Tapes window, load the catalog that contains the files you want to restore. In the Tape File Selection window, select the files you want to restore. Click the appropriate check boxes, and then click the Restore button.
Restore files from a floppy disk to the hard disk	Using Windows NT Explorer or My Computer, drag the files you want to restore from the floppy disk to the location you want on your hard disk.

For online information about	From the Help Topics dialog box, click Index, and then type
Formatting floppy disks	**formatting, disks**
Backing up folders and files	**backup, files**

Review & Practice

You will review and practice how to:

Estimated time
20 min.

- Map a drive to a network computer.
- Make files available to others on your network.
- Send an e-mail message.
- Organize your files and folders.
- Copy and back up files between disks.

You can practice the skills you learned in Part 3 by working through the steps in this Review & Practice section. You will set up and manage a computer filing system, work with files across different disk and network drives, let other people in your organization access files on your computer, communicate with others using electronic mail, and back up files.

Scenario

You have been using your computer and different programs for a while and have generated a number of files associated with different projects. It's now time for others on your team to review your work. You first need to make the files available, and then send a piece of e-mail to members of your team to let them know that your files are ready for their review. While you wait for their comments, you organize and clean up your filing system. You also have files you want to copy between your hard disk and floppy disks.

Step 1:   Create a Review Folder on Your Hard Disk

You want to create a separate folder on your hard disk to contain only the documents you want to be reviewed by other members on your team. In this step, you create a folder called "Review" on your hard disk.

1 Using Windows NT Explorer, create a new folder at the root level (Hint: Select the (C:)\ icon in the All Folders list, and then, on the File menu, click New.)

2 Name the folder Review.

Step 2:   Map To and Open Files on a Network

One of the files you want to include in your review is stored on the network. In this step, you map a drive to one of the computers on your network, and browse through and open shared files available on that computer while looking for a specific file.

1 With the Exploring window still open, map any available computer on your network to a drive on your computer. (Hint: Use the Map Network Drive button on the toolbar.)

2 Open the mapped network drive, and browse through the available folders and files.

3 Locate a document that was created using a program you have set up on your computer, such as WordPad or Paint.

4 Copy the file to the Marketing folder in the Windows NT Practice folder.

5 Close any documents you opened from the network drive.

6 Disconnect from the mapped network drive.

For more information on	See
Using information from network computers	Lesson 7

Step 3:   Designate a Folder as a Shared Resource

You've been working on a number of files in your Marketing folder, and you now want other people on your team to review your work. In this step, you first copy files from your Marketing folder to your Review folder, and then designate the Review folder as a shared resource.

1 Open the Windows NT Practice folder, and then open the Marketing folder.

2 Select all the files.

3   Locate the Review folder, and then place a copy of the selected files in the Review folder. (Hint: Hold down CTRL while dragging the selected files.)

4   Click the Review folder, and then identify the folder as a shared resource with full access. (Hint: Use the Properties command on the File menu.)

5   Close all open windows.

For more information on	See
Making information available on the network	Lesson 7

Step 4:   *Send E-mail Messages*

Now that the Review folder is set up, you need to send e-mail to your team members to let them know that the files are available for their review. In this step, you send an e-mail message using Microsoft Exchange.

1   Use Microsoft Exchange to send an e-mail message to let your team members know that the files are ready for review and where they are located. Address the e-mail message to another user of your electronic mail system, if possible, and send yourself a copy as well. (Hint: Use the Compose menu.)

2   Open and read the e-mail message you sent in step 1.

3   Close all open windows.

For more information on	See
Sending information using Microsoft Exchange	Lesson 7

Step 5:   *Organize Your Hard Disk*

While you wait for review comments, you decide to organize the files on your computer. In this step, you create new folders that reflect your file organization scheme, and then move the files into the appropriate folders.

1   In the Windows NT Practice folder, create the following new folders:

Professional Development
Benefits

2   Move the following files into the indicated folders.

Move this file	To this folder
Brown Bag Presentations	Professional Development
Brown Bag Lunch	Professional Development
New Employees Report	Benefits
Retirement Planning	Benefits

3 Rename the following files as indicated.

In this folder	Rename this file	To this
Professional Development	Brown Bag Presentations	Brown Bag Graphic
Professional Development	Brown Bag Lunch	Brown Bag Flyer
Benefits	Retirement Planning	Stock Option Plan
Letters	Orientation Letter	Welcome Memo

4 In the Windows NT Practice folder, delete the 1990 Employee List.

5 Close all open windows.

For more information on	See
Organizing your files	Lesson 8
Renaming and copying files and folders	Lesson 8
Deleting files and folders	Lesson 8

Step 6: Back Up Files

In this step, you create a new folder on your hard disk, and then copy files into the folder from a floppy disk. You also make a backup of a folder from your hard disk to a floppy disk.

1 Open the Windows NT Practice folder. Create a new folder there, and name it Presentations.

2 Insert the floppy disk labeled "Windows NT Disk Practice," that you created in Lesson 9, into your floppy disk drive.

3 Copy all the files from the floppy disk to the new Presentations folder.

4 Make a backup copy of the Marketing folder on your floppy disk. (Hint: Use the Send To command on the File menu.)

5 Close all open windows.

For more information on	See
Backing up files to a floppy disk	Lesson 9
Backing up files to the network	Lesson 9

Finish the Review & Practice

1 Delete the "Review" folder from your hard disk.

2 Close all open windows by clicking the Close button in the upper-right corner of each window.

Close

3 If any window is minimized, use the right mouse button to click the window's taskbar button, and then click Close.

You are now ready to start the next lesson, or you can work on your own.

4 If you are finished using Windows NT for now, on the Start menu, click Shut Down, and then click Yes.

Getting Connected

Working Away From Your Office

Estimated time
30 min.

In this lesson you will learn how to:

- Synchronize files between your desktop and laptop computers using My Briefcase.
- Set up your office computer to be remotely accessible.
- Dial in to your office computer from your home or laptop computer.

If you use computers in different locations—for example, one at work and one at home—you might work on the same files on both machines. Using My Briefcase, a Windows NT accessory that can help you to store and synchronize files between two computers, you can make sure that you're always working on the most current version of a file you share between the two computers.

You can also use a *modem* and telephone line to connect to your desktop computer when you're away from your office. Or, if you're traveling on business, you can connect to your office computer to access shared files on your company's network.

In this lesson, you'll learn how to efficiently synchronize and access information when you work away from your office computer.

Going Mobile with My Briefcase

You might be traveling as a part of your job or occasionally take work home. When traveling between locations, you might use a briefcase to carry your paper files. In the same way, with Windows NT, you can copy electronic folders and files into My Briefcase.

You can copy the folders and files you want to use on another computer into My Briefcase, move My Briefcase onto a floppy disk, and then use the disk on the other computer. This is useful when you work on the same files using two different computers—for example, your office computer and your home computer, or your desktop computer and your laptop computer.

My Briefcase does more than just transfer files; it also allows you to *synchronize* duplicate files that are stored in two locations. My Briefcase keeps track of the duplicate files, and alerts you when one of the files is different from the other. My Briefcase also prompts you to update a file by replacing the older version with the newer. By using My Briefcase, you can be more confident that your files are current and synchronized properly.

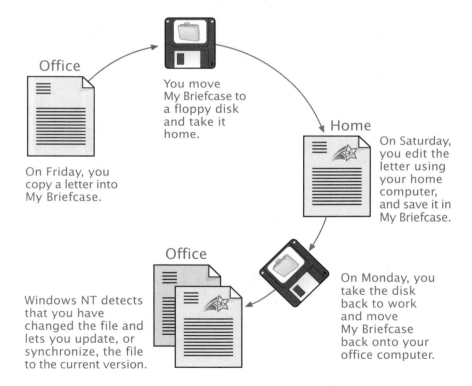

Office

You move My Briefcase to a floppy disk and take it home.

On Friday, you copy a letter into My Briefcase.

Home

On Saturday, you edit the letter using your home computer, and save it in My Briefcase.

Office

Windows NT detects that you have changed the file and lets you update, or synchronize, the file to the current version.

On Monday, you take the disk back to work and move My Briefcase back onto your office computer.

In the following exercises, you will use My Briefcase to copy a set of files, move it to another computer using My Briefcase, edit the files using the other computer, and then synchronize them using My Briefcase.

Copy files into My Briefcase

Suppose you have a computer at home and one at your office, and sometimes bring home some of your office files to work on over the weekend. In this exercise, you copy files located on your office computer into My Briefcase for use on your home computer.

 NOTE Your "home" computer can be any other computer running Windows NT or Windows 95. If another computer is not available, you can use the same computer.

1 If your computer isn't already on, turn it on now. If necessary, press CTRL+ALT+DELETE to log on. Type your password if you're using one, and then press ENTER. If you see the Welcome dialog box, click the Close button.

2 Using Windows NT Explorer, open the Windows NT Practice folder on your hard disk, and then use the right mouse button to drag the Product Table file into My Briefcase.

A shortcut menu appears.

3 On the shortcut menu, click Make Sync Copy.

The Product Table file is copied to My Briefcase.

4 On the Desktop, double-click the My Briefcase icon.

If you see the Welcome To The Windows Briefcase window, read it, and then click Finish. The My Briefcase window appears. Your screen should look similar to the following illustration.

If your screen looks different from this illustration, refer to Appendix B, "Matching the Exercises."

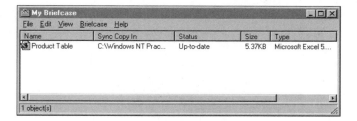

5 On the taskbar, click the Exploring-Windows NT Practice button.

6 Use the right mouse button to drag the Internal folder from the Windows NT Practice folder into the My Briefcase window, and then, on the shortcut menu, click Make Sync Copy.

A synchronized copy of the Internal folder appears in the My Briefcase window.

7 Close the My Briefcase window.

Move My Briefcase to a floppy disk

Now that you have copied the files you want to work on over the weekend into My Briefcase, you need to move them from My Briefcase to a floppy disk so that they can be transferred to your home computer.

 NOTE In the following exercises, you will use the floppy disk that you formatted earlier in Lesson 9, "Backing Up Your Important Information." If you have not done Lesson 9, obtain a formatted floppy disk that you can use in one of your floppy disk drives, and write "Windows NT Disk Practice" on the sticker.

1 Insert the floppy disk labeled "Windows NT Disk Practice" into the appropriate drive of your office computer.

2 On the taskbar, click the Exploring-Windows NT Practice button.

The Exploring window appears.

3 Use the right mouse button to drag the My Briefcase icon from the Desktop to your floppy disk drive icon in Windows NT Explorer.

A shortcut menu appears.

The entire contents of My Briefcase must fit on the disk; it can't extend over multiple disks.

4 On the shortcut menu, click Move Here.

My Briefcase and all the files it contains are moved to the floppy disk. The My Briefcase icon disappears from your Desktop.

5 Double-click the floppy disk drive icon.

The My Briefcase icon appears among the list of items stored on your floppy disk.

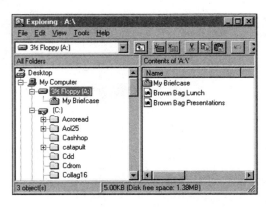

6 Double-click My Briefcase to open it.

The folder and file you copied to My Briefcase appear.

7 Close all open windows.

8 Remove the floppy disk from the drive.

You can now take the files on the Windows NT Disk Practice disk and use them on another computer running Windows NT or Windows 95.

Edit the files in My Briefcase

You are ready to wrap up some of the work you did not have time to finish during the week. In this exercise, you edit one of the files contained in My Briefcase using your home computer.

 NOTE Try the following exercise on another Windows NT or Windows 95 computer. If another computer is not available, you can use the same computer.

1 Insert the floppy disk labeled "Windows NT Disk Practice" into the floppy disk drive of your home computer.

2 Using Windows NT Explorer, open the floppy disk drive.

The My Briefcase icon is displayed in the contents list.

You could also move the My Briefcase icon from the floppy disk to the hard disk to work on the files from your hard disk.

3 Double-click the My Briefcase icon to open it.

4 Double-click the Internal folder to open it.

5 Double-click the 1997 Product Line file to open it in WordPad.

6 At the top of the document, add the following title text:

Childs Play

1997 Product Line

Marketing Proposal

7 On the toolbar, click the Save button.

8 Close the 1997 Product Line document window.

9 Close all open windows, and remove the floppy disk from the disk drive.

Save

Synchronize files so that you work with the most recent version

You are back at your office, and want to make sure that the changes you made on your home computer to the 1997 Product Line file are synchronized with the older version of the 1997 Product Line file on your work computer. In this exercise, you synchronize the files on your office computer with the files stored in My Briefcase.

1 Insert the floppy disk labeled "Windows NT Disk Practice" into the floppy disk drive of your office computer.

2 Using Windows NT Explorer, open the floppy disk drive.

3 Use the right mouse button to drag the My Briefcase icon from the floppy disk drive to an empty area on your Desktop, and then, on the shortcut menu, click Move Here.

   The My Briefcase icon, and the folder and files it contains are moved from the floppy disk to the Desktop.

4 Remove the floppy disk from the disk drive, and then close all open windows.

5 Double-click the My Briefcase icon to open it.

   The folder and files are listed. The Status column for the Internal folder displays "Needs Updating."

6 Double-click the Internal folder.

   The Internal window appears and shows that the 1997 Product Line file needs to be updated.

7 On the Briefcase menu, click Update All.

   The files located in My Briefcase are compared to the corresponding files on your office computer. The Update My Briefcase window appears, indicating that the 1997 Product Line file in My Briefcase has been modified and that it should replace the unmodified version on the hard disk.

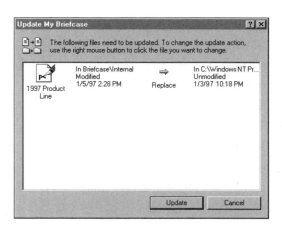

8 Click Update.

   The newer version of the file, located in My Briefcase, replaces the older version located on the hard disk. Now all the files in My Briefcase and on your office computer are synchronized. The Status column displays "Up-To-Date" to confirm that all the files and folders are synchronized and up to date.

9 Close any open windows.

Understanding Telecommunication

You can work with and access other computers by connecting to a network or using *telecommunication* devices. While most networks use network software and cabling to connect computers within a building, telecommunication uses communication software and telephone lines. You can connect your computer to a telephone line, and then call other computers that are also connected to telephone lines.

In order to establish a connection, you must have a *modem* as part of your computer hardware. A modem is a device that links your computer and your telephone line, and converts computer information into signals that can be sent across telephone lines. A modem may be either internal or external. Internal modems are installed inside your computer case, and external modems are separate boxes that are connected to your computer by a cable. The computer you're calling must also be connected to a modem so that it can translate the signals sent through the telephone lines back into computer information. Any computer equipped with a modem and communication software can send information to and receive information from other computers.

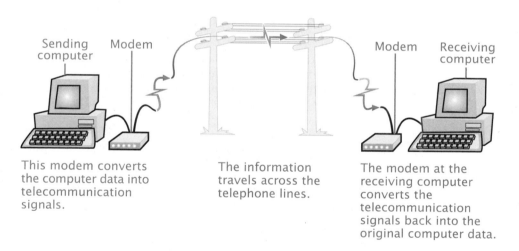

Sending computer Modem   Modem Receiving computer

This modem converts the computer data into telecommunication signals.

The information travels across the telephone lines.

The modem at the receiving computer converts the telecommunication signals back into the original computer data.

IMPORTANT   In order to perform the rest of the exercises in this lesson, you need to have a modem as part of your computer hardware. If you do not have a modem, you can skip the rest of this lesson.

Using Telecommunication to Work Remotely

You can use *Dial-Up Networking* to call another Windows NT or Windows 95 computer. Both computers must have Dial-Up Networking and modems, and the computer you are calling must have dial-up server software. This is particularly useful if you have a Windows NT computer and a modem at home as well as at work. From your home computer, you can use Dial-Up Networking to dial in and connect to your office computer.

In the workplace, this can also be useful if you need to access another Windows NT computer, but the two computers are not on a network. If the computer you want to connect to is equipped with a modem, you can easily call and access it. You might also want to use Dial-Up Networking to print files located on your computer to a printer connected to another Windows NT machine.

 NOTE Dial-Up Networking is an optional accessory that may or may not have been installed on your computer when Microsoft Windows NT was set up. To complete the following exercise, you must have Dial-Up Networking installed. For more information, see "Changing Your Windows NT Workstation Setup" in Appendix A.

Set up a Dial-Up Networking connection to your office computer

Suppose you want to be able to access files located on your work computer from home. In this exercise, you pretend to be working on your home computer, and set up a Dial-Up Networking connection to establish a communication channel between your office computer and your home computer.

1   Open My Computer.
2   In the My Computer window, double-click the Dial-Up Networking icon.

    The Dial-Up Networking window appears.
3   In the Dial-Up Networking window, click New Phonebook Entry.

    The New Phonebook Entry wizard appears.

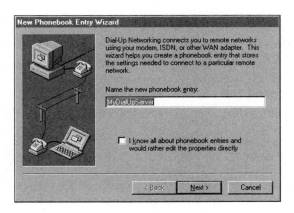

4   In the Computer Name box, type **My Office Computer**

This will be the name of the icon you will double-click every time you want to call this computer.

5   Click Next, and then click Next again.

6   Type the area code for your office computer in the Area Code box, type **555-1111**, and then click Next.

7   In the next window, click Finish.

A new entry named "My Home Computer" appears in the Phonebook Entry To Dial drop-down list.

NOTE   If you haven't connected to another computer before, you may need to specify communication parameters. To do so, click the Configure button next to the Modem list box. In the Modem Properties dialog box, set the communication port, speed, data bits, parity, and stop bits so that they are identical for both computers. The *communication port* indicates which connector on the computer's system unit your modem is using. The rest of these parameters are settings modems use to define how they'll send and receive information. These settings must be identical for both modems in order for them to be able to communicate with each other.

Dial-in to your office computer

Now that you have set up the connection between your home computer and your office computer, suppose you actually want to dial in to your office computer from your home computer. In this exercise, you learn how to call your office computer with Dial-Up Networking.

1   If you plan on calling your office computer from your home computer, be sure to leave your office computer turned on and to verify that you are logged onto Microsoft Windows NT.

2   Open the Dial-Up Networking window, click the Phonebook Entry To Dial down arrow, and then click My Office Computer.

The Connect To dialog box appears.

3   Click Connect.

Your home computer dials your office computer's phone number. If you're using the dummy number, you'll hear the phone number being dialed, and then you'll hear a recorded message saying that the number is not in service. In this case, click Cancel.

4   Close all open windows.

One Step Further: Saving Custom Settings for Your Laptop Docking Station

If you use a laptop computer and a docking station, you can create several *hardware profiles*, a series of custom settings, specific to the different hardware configurations you use. For example, if your laptop computer is docked when you work at your office, you might use a larger keyboard and monitor, and a full-size mouse. In addition, your docked computer uses certain settings to connect to the network and get your e-mail messages. You can create a hardware profile that remembers these settings.

When you work away from your office and use your laptop computer undocked, you usually don't use a full-size monitor, keyboard, or mouse. You also probably use different hardware settings if you check your e-mail or connect to your organization's network from a remote location. You can create a hardware profile that remembers these settings.

If you have created several hardware profiles, you can choose which configuration you want to use each time you start your computer.

 IMPORTANT   In order to perform the following exercises, you need to have a laptop computer and a docking station. If you do not, skip these exercises.

Create a new hardware profile

You are getting ready to go on a business trip during which you will need to connect to your company's network to access information. In order to speed up and simplify your log on procedure, you decide to create a hardware profile. In this exercise, you create a hardware profile for your undocked computer.

1   Remove your laptop computer from the docking station.

2   Use the right mouse button to click the My Computer icon, and then click Properties.

3   In the System Properties dialog box, click the Hardware Profiles tab.

   In the Available Hardware Profiles list, "Original Configuration (Current)" should be highlighted.

4   Click the Copy button.

   This makes a copy of your original hardware profile.

5   In the To box, type **When Laptop Is Undocked**, and then click OK.

6   Click the Properties button.

7   On the General tab, select the This Is A Portable Computer check box. Click The Computer Is Undocked option button, and then click OK.

8   Click OK to close the Hardware Profiles dialog box.

9   Close all other windows.

 NOTE   You can create an additional hardware profile for when your laptop computer is docked by inserting it in its docking station, and then repeating steps 3 through 7. Be sure to type a different descriptive name, and then select the Computer Is Docked option button.

Use your new hardware profile

You are preparing for a meeting while on a business trip, and need to connect to your company's network using your laptop computer. In this exercise, you start your computer using the hardware profile you created in the previous exercise.

1   Restart your computer.

   Microsoft Windows NT restarts and displays the Hardware Profile/Configuration Recovery Menu in MS-DOS mode.

2   Select the When Laptop Is Undocked option using the down arrow key on your keyboard, and then press ENTER.

3   Press CTRL+ALT+DELETE to log on, and then type your password as you normally do.

   Windows NT uses the When Laptop Is Undocked hardware profile.

Finish the lesson

In the following steps, you will return your computer to the settings it had when you started this lesson. You will also close any open windows.

1 Double-click the My Briefcase icon. Hold down SHIFT and click the Internal folder and the Product Table file. On the Briefcase menu, click Split From Original, and then click Yes. Then, drag the Internal folder and Product Table file to Recycle Bin.

   The items are deleted from My Briefcase.

2 If you did the One Step Further exercise, restart your computer and choose the Original Configuration hardware profile. Log on to your computer as you normally do. If you see the Welcome dialog box, click Close.

3 If you did the One Step Further exercise, use the right mouse button to click My Computer, and then click Properties. Click the Hardware Profiles button. In the Available Hardware Profiles list, click When Laptop Is Undocked, and then click Delete. Click OK to close the Hardware Profiles and System dialog boxes.

| ☒ |
| Close |

4 Close any open windows by clicking the Close button in the upper-right corner of each window.

   You are now ready to start the next lesson, or you can work on your own.

5 If you are finished using Windows NT for now, on the Start menu, click Shut Down, and then click Yes.

Lesson Summary

To	Do this
Make a synchronized copy of files or folders with My Briefcase	Drag the files or folders to the My Briefcase icon.
Move My Briefcase to a floppy disk	Insert a disk in the floppy disk drive. Using Windows NT Explorer, move the My Briefcase icon to the floppy disk drive icon.
Use files stored in My Briefcase on another computer	Insert the floppy disk, open the drive, and then open My Briefcase.
Update files between your computer and My Briefcase	Open My Briefcase. On the Briefcase menu, click Update All, and then click Update.

To	Do this
Establish a new Dial-Up Networking connection	Double-click My Computer, and then double-click the Dial-Up Networking icon, click New, and follow the New Phonebook Entry Wizard to establish the new connection.
Call another computer using Dial-Up Networking	Be sure that the computer you are calling is on and the connection is open. In My Computer, double-click Dial-Up Networking. Click the entry for the connection in the drop-down list, and then click Dial.
Create a hardware profile	With the right mouse button, click My Computer, and then click Properties. Click the Hardware Profiles tab.

For online information about	From the Help Topics dialog box, click Index, and then type
Using My Briefcase	**My Briefcase**
Connecting to a computer from a remote location	**Dialing Another Computer, By Using Dial-Up Networking**
Creating a hardware profile	**hardware profile**

Tapping Into a World of Information

Estimated time
40 min.

In this lesson you will learn how to:

- Explore the Internet using Microsoft Internet Explorer.
- Connect to a bulletin board using Microsoft HyperTerminal.

If your computer has a modem, you can access a whole world of information outside your organization. Through your computer, you can look for information that can help you solve problems, or can spark your professional or personal interests. You can also get in contact with people from around the world and share ideas with them. In this lesson, you'll learn some of the ways you can connect with other people and get access to information through online services, the Internet, and bulletin board services.

Exploring the Internet

Microsoft Windows NT includes an accessory called Internet Explorer that you can use to browse the Internet. The Internet connects computers and networks from around the world, and makes information on every subject you can think of available online. The most commonly known part of the Internet is referred to as the *World Wide Web*. It is composed of a multitude of *web sites* which are collections of text, pictures, sounds and digital movies. Each web site is made of a series of customized *web pages*. Web pages contain text, graphics, and links to other web pages that contain related information. It is easy for the author to change the contents of a web page, so it's possible for the same web page to look different or contain different information from one day to the next.

NOTE In order to perform the following exercises, you must have a modem and access to the Internet through your organization's network or another Internet service provider. If you're not sure whether or not you have access to the Internet, ask your system administrator.

Browse the Internet with Internet Explorer

In this exercise, you start browsing the Internet using Internet Explorer.

Internet Explorer

1 Double-click the Internet Explorer icon on your Desktop.

Once you're connected, Internet Explorer displays The Microsoft Internet Explorer start page which provides tools to help you explore the Internet. You'll see words and phrases that are colored and underlined, and you'll notice that your mouse pointer changes shape when you move it over them; this is also true for pictures displayed on web pages. These words, phrases, and pictures are called *hyperlinks* or *hot links,* and when you click them once with your mouse, you jump to another spot on the same web page or on a related web page.

2 Scroll down to the bottom of the page, and then click the text http://www.msn.com

The colored text is a hyperlink that takes you to the Microsoft Network start page. The appearance of the start page can change dramatically, but your screen might look similar to the following illustration.

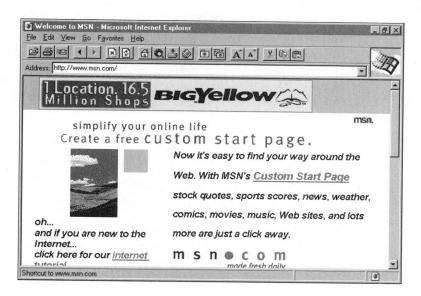

3 Scroll down and click the word Search.

The Internet Searches page appears and lists a number of search services that you can use to find things on the Internet.

4 Click in the box, and then type **Library of Congress** to find call numbers, descriptions, and other information on books cataloged in the Library of Congress.

5 Click the Search button.

After a few moments, a list of categories of books cataloged in the Library of Congress appears.

6 Scroll through the list, reading the summary of each web page until you see a category that interests you, and then place your mouse pointer over a category with colored text.

The shape of the pointer changes to a hand to indicate that your pointer is placed on a hot link.

7 Click the hyperlink for the category that interests you.

Internet Explorer displays the web page.

Back

8 On the toolbar, click the Back button to go back to the list of book categories in the Library of Congress.

9 On the toolbar, click the Open Start Page button to go back to the Microsoft Internet Explorer start page.

Open Start Page

10 Scroll down to The Microsoft Network hot link, and then click on it to return to The Microsoft Network start page.

199

Speed up the display of a web page

Sometimes you can speed up the display of web pages by turning off certain options. When you turn these options off, web pages will not display large pictures, animation, or sound; they will only display text. This is useful when you need to quickly search a number of different Web pages for textual information.

1   With the Microsoft Network window open, on the View menu, click Options, and then click the Appearance tab, if necessary.

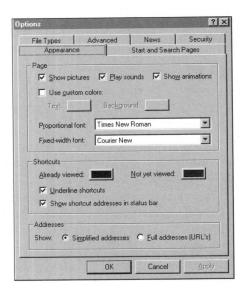

2   Clear the Show Pictures, Play Sounds, and Show Animations check boxes, and then click OK.

3   On the Microsoft Network start page, click Microsoft Products.

Internet Explorer displays the Microsoft Products web page, without displaying pictures.

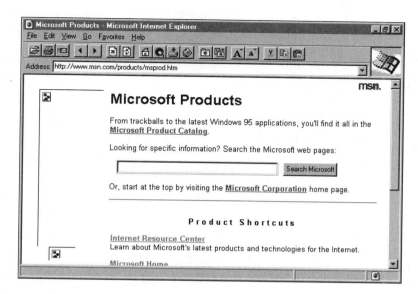

4 On the Microsoft Products web page, click Microsoft Product Catalog.

Internet Explorer displays the Microsoft Product Catalog web page. You can see the product descriptions, but you don't see any pictures.

5 On the toolbar, click the Back button.

6 On the View menu, click Options, and then click the Appearance tab.

7 Select the Show Pictures, Play Sounds, and Show Animations check boxes, and then click OK.

8 On the Microsoft Products web page, click Microsoft Product Catalog.

Now you can see the pictures in the Microsoft Product Catalog, although it probably took longer to display the web page.

9 On the toolbar, click Open Start Page.

Go directly to a web page by typing the address

If you know the address of a web page, you can go there directly without having to conduct a search. In this exercise, you type in the address of the Microsoft Windows NT product support web page.

NOTE You may occasionally get an error message informing you that the web page you're trying to display is not available. If you run into such an error, click the Back button, the Home Page button, or on the File menu, click Exit.

1 With the Internet Explorer window open, on the File menu, click Open.

The Open Internet Address dialog box appears.

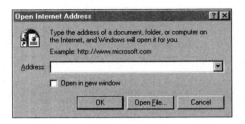

2 In the Address box, type **http://www.microsoft.com/support/products/ backoffice/winnt.htm**

3 Select the Open In New Window check box.

4 Click OK to get the latest product support information for Windows NT.

The Microsoft Support Online for Windows NT Server and Workstation web page appears in a new window.

5 On the File menu, click Exit.

You're disconnected from the Internet.

Connecting to a Bulletin Board

Microsoft HyperTerminal is an accessory that allows you to call and log on to a bulletin board service. A *bulletin board service (BBS)* is a type of online service with a narrower scope than the Internet, usually established for a special interest and a defined membership. There are bulletin board services that are accessed by calling a designated BBS computer and that are set up specifically to provide certain types of technical information, job searches in a particular field, information on a professional organization, and so on. Some of these services are free; some services assess service charges and/or long-distance phone charges. Always read introductory BBS screens carefully for an explanation of charges.

In the following exercises, you set up your modem connections, and then connect your computer to a free BBS offered by Microsoft and named the Microsoft Download Service. It provides information about Microsoft programs, such as Microsoft Word, Microsoft Excel, and Microsoft Works.

Specify a HyperTerminal connection to another computer

Suppose you want to call a computer bulletin board service. In this exercise, you set up your modem connections and prepare your computer to call a BBS called the Microsoft Download Service.

1   Click Start. Point to Programs, and then point to Accessories.

2   On the Accessories menu, point to the HyperTerminal folder, and then click HyperTerminal.

First, the New Connection-HyperTerminal window appears, and then the Connection Description dialog box appears. Your screen should look similar to the following illustration.

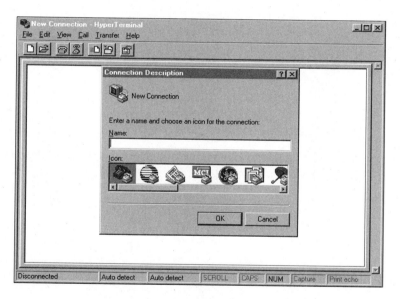

3   In the Name box, type **Microsoft Download Service**

The first icon on the left of the Icon list box is already selected. This icon will represent the Microsoft Download Service in the HyperTerminal window, and will be named using the name you have specified.

4   Click OK.

The Connect To dialog box appears.

5 In the Area code box, type **206**, if necessary.

6 In the Phone Number box, type **936-6735**

This number is in Washington state. If you prefer to use a "dummy" phone number, for practice only, you can type **555-2222**, and then click OK.

7 Click OK.

The Connect dialog box appears.

Dial another computer using HyperTerminal

Now that you have defined your settings, you're ready to make the connection. In this exercise, you call and connect to the Microsoft Download Service.

1 In the Connect dialog box, click Dialing Properties.

The Dialing Properties dialog box appears.

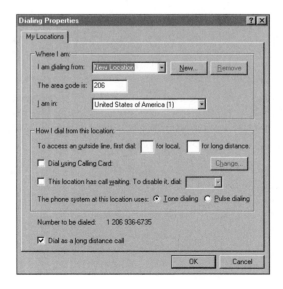

2 At the bottom of the Dialing Properties dialog box, verify that the Dial As A Long Distance Call check box is selected, if applicable.

3 If you use a number such as "1" or "9" to access an outside line, enter it in the appropriate box, and then click OK.

The Connect dialog box reappears.

4 Click the Dial button.

After a few moments, the Microsoft Download Service-HyperTerminal window appears. If you used the "dummy" phone number, you'll hear a recorded message saying that the number is not in service.

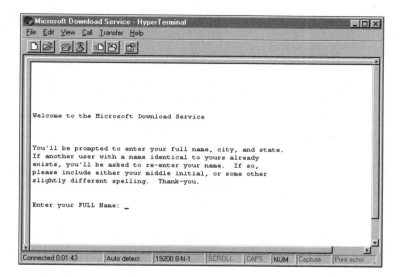

5 Follow the instructions displayed on the screen to sign up for the Microsoft Download Service.

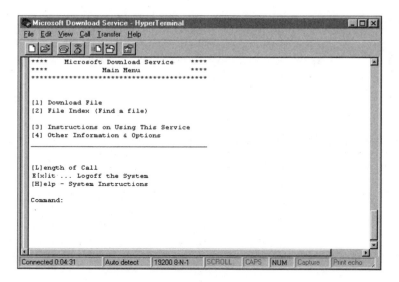

6 At the Command prompt of the Microsoft Download Service Main Menu, type **X** to exit the Microsoft Download Service.

 TIP You can find the names, numbers, and descriptions of other computer bulletin board services in your local computer newspaper or in your favorite computer magazines.

Save the HyperTerminal connection settings

Suppose you expect to dial into this bulletin board frequently and you want to be able to do this without having to type in the phone number and other communication settings each time. In this exercise, you save your connection settings as a file.

1 On the File menu of the Microsoft Download Service-HyperTerminal window, click Save.

2 Close the Microsoft Download Service-HyperTerminal window.

3 Close all open windows.

One Step Further: Using Shortcuts to Access Your Favorite Web Pages Quickly

If you use a certain web page often, you can create a shortcut on your Desktop to access the page directly without having to type in its address each time you want to view it.

NOTE This exercise assumes that you have joined The Microsoft Network or that your organization has direct access to the Internet.

Create a Desktop shortcut to a web page you use often

1 Double-click The Internet Explorer icon.

2 On the File menu, click Open.

3 Type **http://www.microsoft.com/MSOffice/msofc/fs_ofc.htm**, and then click OK.

The Microsoft Office Home Page appears.

4 On the File menu, click Create Shortcut.

Internet Explorer displays a message informing you that a shortcut to the current page will be placed on your Desktop.

5 Click OK.

6 On the File menu, click Exit.

A shortcut to the Microsoft Office Home Page appears on your Desktop.

7 Double-click the Microsoft Office Home Page shortcut.

Internet Explorer goes directly to and displays the Microsoft Office Home Page.

8 On the File menu, click Exit.

Finish the lesson

In the following steps, you will return your computer to the settings it had when you started this lesson. You will also close any open windows.

1   Click Start. Point to Settings, and click Taskbar. Click the Start Menu Programs tab. Click Remove. Double-click the Accessories menu. Double-click the HyperTerminal folder. Select the Microsoft Download Service icon, and then click Remove. Click Yes in the Confirm File Delete dialog box.

2   Drag the shortcut to the Microsoft Office Home Page located on your Desktop to the Recycle Bin icon.

Close

3   Close all open windows by clicking the Close button in the upper-right corner of each window.

You are now ready to start the Review & Practice section, or you can work on your own.

4   If you are finished using Windows NT for now, on the Start menu, click Shut Down, and then click Yes.

Lesson Summary

To	Do this
Browse the Internet	On your Desktop, double-click the Internet Explorer icon. Click the hyperlink to www.msn.com, and then click Searches.
Speed up the display of a web page	In Internet Explorer, on the View menu, click Options. Clear the Show Pictures, Play Sounds, and Show Animations check boxes.
Go directly to a web page by typing the address	In Internet Explorer, on the File menu, click Open. Type the address of the web page you want to go to.
Connect to another computer using HyperTerminal	Click Start. Point to Programs, point to Accessories, and then click HyperTerminal. Type a connection name, select an icon, and then click OK. Enter the phone number, click OK, and then click Dial.
Save the HyperTerminal connection settings	On the File menu of the HyperTerminal window, click Save.

To	Do this
Dial a saved HyperTerminal connection	Click Start. Point to Programs, point to Accessories, point to HyperTerminal, and then click the icon for the appropriate saved connection.
Create a Desktop shortcut to a web page you use often	In Internet Explorer, display the page you want. On the File menu, click Create Shortcut.

For online information about	From the Help Topics dialog box, click Index, and then type
Connecting to the Internet	**Internet**
Connecting to other computers using HyperTerminal	**HyperTerminal**

Review & Practice

You will review and practice how to:

■ Connect to a bulletin board.

■ Synchronize files using My Briefcase.

You can practice the skills you learned in Part 4 by working through the steps in this Review & Practice section. You will work with other computers using file synchronization and telephone connections.

Scenario

You're going on a business trip to meet with important clients and attend a professional conference. You need to prepare files to take with you and use on your laptop computer. Once at your destination, you'll use your modem to call the Childs Play bulletin board and download some additional information you'll need for a client presentation.

Step 1: Copy Files to My Briefcase

You need to take all the files in the Marketing and Letters folders with you on your business trip. You also want to be sure that you'll be able to synchronize any files you have modified upon your return. In this step, you copy the two folders from your work computer to My Briefcase, and then move My Briefcase to a floppy disk to be taken with you and used on your laptop computer.

1   From the Windows NT Practice folder, make a synchronized copy of the Marketing and Letters folders, including all subfolders and files, in My Briefcase. (Hint: Use the right mouse button to drag the folders from Windows NT Explorer to the My Briefcase icon on your Desktop. On the shortcut menu, click Make Sync Copy.)

2   Move My Briefcase to your floppy disk labeled "Windows NT Disk Practice."

3   Remove the floppy disk from the disk drive.

For more information on	See
Using My Briefcase	Lesson 10

Step 2:   *Edit the My Briefcase Files*

You're now on the road, and you've finished your first day of meetings. Based on the outcome of those meetings, you update the files you've brought with you in My Briefcase.

 NOTE   Try the following exercise on another computer running Windows NT or Windows 95, if available. Otherwise, you can use the same computer.

1   Insert the floppy disk labeled "Windows NT Disk Practice" into your disk drive.

2   Use Windows NT Explorer to move My Briefcase from the floppy disk to your Desktop.

3   Open My Briefcase.

4   Open the Marketing folder, and then open the WordPad document named Marketing Proposal. Under the Budget section (toward the bottom of the document), type the following paragraph.

    Based on discussions with the southwest regional distributors and retail outlets, we have developed the following budgetary estimates for marketing and sales.

5   Save and close the document.

6   Close My Briefcase.

7   Move My Briefcase from the Desktop to your floppy disk.

8   Remove the floppy disk from the disk drive.

9   Close all open windows.

For more information on	See
Using My Briefcase	Lesson 10

Step 3:   *Using a Phone to connect to Another Computer*

While meeting with your clients, you need to get some additional information that is available on the Childs Play bulletin board. In this step, you establish a connection and log on to the BBS.

 IMPORTANT   You must have a modem installed on your computer in order to complete this exercise.

1   Start the HyperTerminal accessory.

2   Create a connection to the Childs Play Bulletin Board using the 555-3333 phone number.

3   Dial the new computer connection, and then cancel it.

4   Save the new connection.

5   Close all open windows.

For more information on	See
Connecting to a Bulletin Board	Lesson 11

Step 4:   *Synchronize Files with My Briefcase*

Back in your office after your trip, you need to synchronize the files you used on your laptop computer with the corresponding files stored on your desktop computer. In this step, you use My Briefcase to update the files on your desktop computer.

1   Insert the floppy disk labeled "Windows NT Disk Practice" into your disk drive.

2   Use Windows NT Explorer to display the content of the floppy disk.

3   Move My Briefcase from the floppy disk to your Desktop.

4   Open My Briefcase and locate the files that need updating. (Hint: Double-click the My Briefcase icon, and then look in the Status column.)

5   Update each of the files as required to synchronize the changed file in My Briefcase with the corresponding file on your hard disk.

6   Close all open windows.

For more information on	See
Using My Briefcase	Lesson 10

Finish the Review & Practice

In the following steps, you will return your computer to the settings it had when you started this Review and Practice. You will also close any open windows.

1   Double-click the My Briefcase icon. Hold down SHIFT and click the Letters and Marketing folders so that both are selected. On the Briefcase menu, click Split From Original, and then click Yes. Drag the Letters and Marketing folders to Recycle Bin.

2   On the Start menu, point to Programs, point to Accessories, point to HyperTerminal, and then click the Childs Play Bulletin Board icon. Click the Childs Play Bulletin Board icon. On the File menu, click Delete, and then click Yes.

3   Close all open windows by clicking the Close button in the upper-right corner of each window.

4   If any window is minimized, use the right mouse button to click the window's taskbar button, and then click Close.

You are now ready to work on your own.

5   If you are finished using Windows NT for now, on the Start menu, click Shut Down, and then click Yes.

Appendixes

Appendix A

Installing Microsoft Windows NT Workstation

In Appendix A you will learn how to:

- Prepare your system before installing Windows NT Workstation.
- Install Windows NT Workstation on your computer.
- Change your setup after installing Windows NT Workstation.

Whether or not you have a previous version of Microsoft Windows NT installed on your computer, this appendix will guide you through installing Microsoft Windows NT Workstation version 4.0.

 NOTE If you have previously installed Microsoft Windows 95 on your computer, you cannot upgrade it to Microsoft Windows NT Workstation version 4.0. You must install Windows NT Workstation version 4.0 in a separate folder, and your computer will *dual-boot*, meaning that when you start your computer, you will have to choose which operating system you want to use.

If you already have Microsoft Windows NT Workstation version 4.0 set up on your computer, this appendix can also help you set up your printer or additional programs.

NOTE For specific setup procedures and more detailed technical information, see the *Start Here: Basics and Installation* book, which comes with Microsoft Windows NT Workstation version 4.0.

Preparing Your System for Microsoft Windows NT Workstation

Before you install Microsoft Windows NT Workstation, be sure that your computer system includes at least the minimum system requirements and that you know your hardware components and current settings. If you're upgrading a computer that has important files stored on the hard disk, make backup copies of those files.

Hardware Requirements

To run Microsoft Windows NT Workstation version 4.0, your computer system must have the following components:

- A 32-bit 80486 or better-based microprocessor (such as Intel 80486/25 or higher), Intel Pentium, or supported RISC-based microprocessor such as Digital Alpha Systems, or PowerPC.
- One or more hard disks with 118 MB minimum free disk space on the partition that will contain the Windows NT Workstation system files (149 MB minimum for RISC-based computers).
- A high density 3.5-inch disk drive plus a CD-ROM drive for 80486 or better-compatible computers. (For computers with only a 5.25-inch drive, you can only install Windows NT Workstation version 4.0 over a network.)
- 12 MB of memory minimum for 80486 or better-based systems; 16 MB is recommended for good performance. (16 MB of memory minimum for RISC-based systems.)
- A standard VGA or higher resolution monitor.
- A mouse or other compatible pointing device.
- One or more network adapter cards if you want to use Windows NT Workstation version 4.0 with a network.
- For any computer not installing over a network, a CD-ROM drive is required.

Before You Install Windows NT Workstation Version 4.0

After you've verified your hardware requirements, the following additional steps are recommended.

- Be sure you read any README files that are on your setup disks. These files contain important information about installing Windows NT Workstation that you usually can't find anywhere else. Also, read the documentation that came with Windows NT Workstation pertaining to setup.

- Back up all of your important data files. You can also back up your program files, if you want.

- Note your hardware settings if you want to preserve them in Windows NT Workstation version 4.0. To do this, you could print your AUTOEXEC.BAT and CONFIG.SYS files, or save them on a floppy disk. Also, if you're upgrading from Windows 3.11 or Windows NT 3.5x, note your hardware settings from Windows Setup (in your Main program group), and note your port, printer, and driver settings.

- Check all of your hardware (network adapter cards, video drivers, sound cards, CD-ROM drives, etc.) against the *Windows NT Hardware Compatibility List*. A copy of this list is included in your Microsoft Windows NT Workstation version 4.0 package. The most up-to-date version of this list is available on the World Wide Web at http://www.microsoft.com/ntserver/hcl/hclinto.htm and on Microsoft's FTP server at ftp://microsoft.com/bussys/winnt/winnt_docs/hcl

- Ensure that you have all the device driver disks and configuration settings for your third-party hardware.

- Label a blank, 3.5-inch 1.44 MB floppy disk with the words "Emergency Repair Disk" and set it aside until Setup asks you to insert it.

- If you will be using your computer on a network, be sure that you know the computer name, workgroup/domain name, and IP address for your computer. If you're not sure, ask your system administrator.

Choosing a File System for the Windows NT Workstation Version 4.0 Disk Partition

The disk space on your hard disk is divided into usable areas called *partitions*. Before the Setup program can install the Windows NT Workstation version 4.0 system files, it must know how you want to partition your hard disk. The partition where you store the Microsoft Windows NT Workstation system files must be on a permanent hard disk and must have enough free disk space to hold all the files. Refer to the "Hardware Requirements" section, earlier in this appendix, for more information.

After you have selected a partition for installing Windows NT Workstation, you must tell Setup which file system—NTFS or FAT—to use with the partition. Make sure you know all the considerations when choosing one file system over another. For more detailed technical information, see the *Start Here: Basics and Installation* book, which comes with Windows NT Workstation version 4.0. In general, keep these points in mind:

- For a new computer that does not contain files you want to preserve, you can choose to format it with either the NTFS or FAT file system. Choose the FAT option if you want access to files on that partition when running Windows NT Workstation, MS-DOS, Windows 95, or OS/2 on this computer. Choose the NTFS option if you plan to only use the Microsoft Windows NT Workstation operating system and want to take advantage of all the security and other Windows NT-specific options.

- If you have a previous version of Microsoft Windows NT Workstation installed on your computer, including an existing disk partition, the default option keeps the current file system intact, preserving all existing files on that partition.

The following table summarizes the main criteria for selecting the appropriate file system for a Windows NT Workstation partition.

	NTFS file system	FAT file system
Security	Supports complete Windows NT security, so you can specify who is allowed various kinds of access to a file or folder.	Files are not protected by the security features of Windows NT.
Activity log	Keeps a log of activities to restore the disk in the event of power failure or other problems.	Does not keep a log.
File size	Maximum file size is 4 GB to 64 GB.	Maximum file size is 4 GB.
File compression	Supports flexible per-file compression.	Doesn't support file compression.
Operating system compatibility	Recognized only by Windows NT. When the computer is running another operating system (such as OS/2), that operating system cannot access files on an NTFS partition on the same computer.	Allows access to files when your computer is running another operating system, such as MS-DOS or OS/2.
MS-DOS data sharing	Cannot share data with MS-DOS on the same partition.	Enables you to share data with MS-DOS on the same partition.

Choosing Your Setup Options

Setup offers four types of installation: Typical, Portable, Compact, or Custom. (The lessons in this book assume a Typical setup. See the Typical description that follows.)

The Typical setup installs the standard components of Windows NT Workstation, including all the components necessary to complete the exercises in this book. "Typical" setup asks you the minimum number of questions and installs all optional Windows NT Workstation components, such as Microsoft Exchange, Internet Explorer, and HyperTerminal. Wherever possible, Typical setup automatically configures the settings for your hardware and other components. Typical setup is the easiest way to install Microsoft Windows NT Workstation and is recommended for users of this book.

The Portable setup installs those components that are useful for laptop, notebook, or other portable computers.

The Compact setup installs only those components that are absolutely essential for Windows NT Workstation to run properly. Use this setup if you have limited disk space on your computer.

The Custom setup is designed for experienced users who want or need more control over how Microsoft Windows NT Workstation is installed on their computers. Custom setup installs only those components that you specifically select. When you choose a Custom setup, you will see a list of program components that you can elect to install or not on your computer.

Installing Windows NT Workstation Version 4.0

You install Windows NT Workstation version 4.0 using the CD-ROM; you can also install it over a network. With either method, you use the Setup program to start the installation.

If you're installing from floppy disks or the CD-ROM, the Setup program starts on the floppy disk labeled "Setup Boot Disk." Setup will prompt you to insert the other floppy disks or the CD-ROM at the appropriate time.

If your organization has a network, your system administrator may have put the Windows NT Workstation program on the network, and you can install it from there. If you're installing from a network location, run the Setup program from the Windows NT Workstation installation folder. The full name of the Setup program is Setup.exe.

After you start the installation, the Setup program will guide you through these phases:

- Detecting the mass storage devices (such as a CD-ROM drive) and verifying other hardware you have installed on your computer system. Setup also asks you specific questions about how you want to configure the disk partitions on your computer and the name of the folder where you want to install the Windows NT Workstation system files.

- Selecting the setup type you want: Typical, Portable, Compact, or Custom.

- Decompressing and copying Windows NT Workstation program files from the CD-ROM or network to your hard disk.

■ Restarting and configuring your Windows NT Workstation version 4.0 system for use.

Install Windows NT Workstation on a 80486 or better-based computer

1 With your computer turned off, insert the floppy disk labeled "Windows NT Setup Boot Disk" into drive A or drive B of your computer.

2 Turn on your computer.

If you're installing on an 80486 or better-based computer, the Setup program automatically starts. After Setup is started, follow the instructions on the screen. When setup is complete, the Welcome dialog box appears.

Install Windows NT Workstation on a RISC-based computer

1 With your computer turned off, insert the floppy disk labeled "Windows NT Setup Boot Disk" into drive A or drive B of your computer.

2 Turn on your computer.

3 At the ARC screen, choose Install Windows NT from CD-ROM Windows NT Setup.

If this choice is not available, choose Run A Program from the menu, and then continue to step 4.

4 At the prompt, type **cd:***system***setupldr**, and then press ENTER, where *system* is the folder name matching your system type: MIPS, i386, PPC (for PowerPC computers), or ALPHA.

For some RISC-based computers, you might need to supply a full device name instead of typing **cd:** See your computer documentation for more information. After Setup is started, follow the instructions on the screen. When Setup is complete, the Welcome dialog box appears.

Install Windows NT Workstation from a network location

1 Using your existing operating system or an MS-DOS disk, establish your connection to the network location where the Setup files are stored.

2 If your computer is currently running a previous version of Microsoft Windows NT, type **winnt32** at the command prompt. For all other installations, type **winnt**

Setup begins with a brief welcome screen asking you to define the process by which you want to proceed with the installation. If you are installing Windows NT Workstation version 4.0 on your machine for the first time, press ENTER to begin the Setup process.

Once Setup is started, follow the instructions on the screen. When Setup is complete, the Welcome dialog box appears.

Preparing to Use Windows NT Workstation Version 4.0

After Windows NT Workstation is fully installed and running on your computer, there are a few more tasks that you will need to perform to make Windows NT Workstation operate properly.

Creating the Find Help Database

The first time you use the Find tab in the Help Topics dialog box, you are prompted to create the "word list" for the Help files. This list contains every word from your Help files. It's a good idea to create the Find list right after you install Windows NT Workstation. This way, when you need to use the Find tab to find a specific Help topic, you won't have to wait for the list to be created.

Load the Find Help database

1   Click Start. On the Start menu, click Help.

    The Help Topics dialog box appears.

2   Click the Find tab.

    The Find tab appears, and then the Find Setup Wizard appears.

3   Read the wizard screen, select the best option for your system, and then click Next.

    The second wizard screen appears.

4   Read the wizard screen, and then click Finish.

    Windows NT creates the search index for your Help files. This process takes a few minutes.

5   Click Cancel to close the Help Topics dialog box.

Installing Your Windows NT-Based Programs

Whether you're working on a brand new computer or you're upgrading your present computer, you'll probably want to install Windows NT-based programs so that you can use them with Windows NT Workstation.

> **NOTE** If you upgrade your existing version of Windows NT Workstation to Windows NT Workstation version 4.0, you do not need to reinstall your programs.

When you want to install a new program for use with Windows NT Workstation, use the Add/Remove Programs icon in Control Panel; it finds the setup program and starts it for you.

Install a Windows NT-based program using Add/Remove Programs

Add/Remove Programs

You can also find Control Panel by clicking Start, and then pointing to Settings.

1   Double-click the My Computer icon.

2   In the My Computer window, double-click the Control Panel icon.

3   In the Control Panel window, double-click the Add/Remove Programs icon.

The Add/Remove Programs Properties dialog box appears. Be sure that the Install/Uninstall tab is active, as shown in the following illustration.

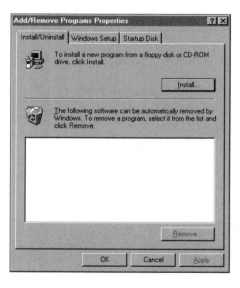

4   Click the Install button.

If you are installing the program from a CD-ROM, you are prompted to insert the CD-ROM into the CD-ROM disk drive. If you are installing the program from a network location, you will be asked to type the correct path for the network location where the program is stored.

5   Find the setup disk (usually Disk 1) of the new application you want to install, and then insert the disk into the appropriate floppy or CD-ROM disk drive.

6   Click the Next button.

Add/Remove Programs searches for the setup program on the disk.

7   After it finds the program, click the Finish button.

8   Continue to answer questions about the program setup.

The program is copied to your hard disk. Follow the instructions on your screen until the program is installed on your computer.

Changing Your Windows NT Workstation Version 4.0 Setup

You can make changes to your Windows NT Workstation version 4.0 setup, even after you have finished the Windows NT Workstation setup. You can add and remove Windows NT Workstation program components with Add/Remove Programs. You can add and remove printers with the Printers utility.

Add or remove Windows NT Workstation components

Regardless of which setup option you choose, you can add or remove components later, after Windows NT Workstation is installed and running. You do not have to run the Setup program again. You can add or remove Windows NT Workstation components with Add/Remove Programs in Windows NT Workstation Control Panel.

1   Double-click the My Computer icon.

2   In the My Computer window, double-click the Control Panel icon.

3   In the Control Panel window, double-click the Add/Remove Programs icon.

The Add/Remove Programs Properties dialog box appears.

4   Click the Windows NT Setup tab to make it active.

5   In the Components list box, double-click a component group, such as Accessories.

The list box displays a detailed list of components in the group. Some groups might only contain one element.

6 Select or clear the check boxes corresponding to the components you want to add or remove. If you are adding a component, you might be prompted to insert the Windows NT CD-ROM. If you originally installed Windows NT Workstation from a network location, you may be prompted to type the path for the network location where the Windows NT Workstation program is stored. Follow the directions on your screen to add the component.

A cleared check box indicates that the component is not installed or will be removed. A selected check box indicates that the component is already installed or will be added. A grayed box indicates that some, but not all, of the components are installed or will be added.

7 Click OK to return to the Windows NT Setup tab to select another component group or to exit Add/Remove Programs.

Install a new printer

You can install a new printer on your computer system to be recognized and used by Windows NT Workstation, without running Windows NT Setup again.

1 Double-click the My Computer icon.

2 In the My Computer window, double-click the Printers folder.

Printers

The Printers window appears. All printers installed with your computer are displayed as named icons.

You can also open the Printers window by clicking Start, pointing to Settings, and then clicking Printers.

3 Double-click the Add Printer icon to display the Add Printer Wizard.

4 Read the information on the Add Printer Wizard's first screen, and then click Next.

The second screen of the Add Printer Wizard appears.

5 Continue to follow the directions listed on the Add Printer Wizard screens to select and add the new printer. You will need to specify the printer model, the port name, and the printer name you want to use. You will also need to insert specified Windows NT Setup disks to obtain the driver files for your particular printer model.

When you are finished, a new icon appears in the Printers window, indicating that your printer has been installed.

Close

6 Close all open windows by clicking the Close button in the upper-right corner of each window.

Matching the Exercises

Microsoft Windows NT Workstation has many optional settings that can affect either the screen display or the operation of certain functions. Some exercise steps, therefore, might not produce exactly the same result on your screen as is shown in this book. If your screen does not look like an illustration at a certain point in a lesson, a note in the lesson might direct you to this appendix for guidance. Or, if you do not get the outcome described in the lesson, you can use this appendix to determine whether the options you have selected are the same as the ones used in this book.

 NOTE Since each computer system is configured with different hardware and software, your screen display of icons, folders, and menu options might not exactly match the illustrations in this book. Such system differences should not interfere with your ability to perform the exercises in the book.

Installing Windows NT Components

The exercises in this book assume a "Typical" setup. If Windows NT was installed on your computer under a "Portable," "Custom," or "Compact" setup, you might not have all the components necessary to complete the lessons.

If you are missing one or two components, such as an accessory, you can easily add it. For instructions on doing this, see the "Changing Your Setup" section in Appendix A, "Installing Windows NT Workstation version 4.0."

Using the Default Windows NT Settings

Windows NT makes it easy for you to configure your Desktop to suit your working style and preferences. However, the exercises in this book assume that all Windows NT options are at their default settings. Even when an exercise changes an option setting, the "Finish the Lesson" procedure usually resets the setting to the default.

You can easily change your Windows NT options to match the illustrations in the exercises.

Show or hide toolbars

You can toggle the toolbar on and off in the My Computer and Windows NT Explorer windows. The toolbar setting can be different for each window that you open. You can show or hide the toolbar on your screen to match the illustrations in this book.

1   On the My Computer or Windows NT Explorer window, click the View menu.

    If the Toolbar command is checked, the toolbar is currently showing; if it is not checked, the toolbar is hidden.

2   On the View menu, click Toolbar to show or hide the toolbar.

Change window sizes

If the size of your windows appear to be different from the exercise illustrations, you can adjust them.

1   Position your mouse pointer on any edge of the window whose size you want to change.

    The mouse pointer changes to a double-headed arrow. You can change the window size horizontally by dragging on a side edge, or vertically by dragging on the top or bottom, or both at the same time by dragging on a corner.

2   Drag the edge or corner of the window in or out to make the window smaller or larger.

Restore windows

If a window fills up the entire screen and you want to see other parts of the Windows NT Desktop, you can restore the window to its previous size.

1   Bring the maximized window to the top of your Desktop by clicking its button on the taskbar.

Restore

2 On the maximized window, click the Restore button in the upper-right corner.

The window is restored to its previous, smaller size.

Change views

If the way files appear in a My Computer or Windows NT Explorer window are different from the illustrations in the book, you can change the view. The views can be different for each My Computer window that you open. You can change the view on your computer to match the illustrations in this book.

1 In the My Computer or Windows NT Explorer window for which you want to change the view, click the View menu.

2 On the View menu, click the appropriate view: Large Icons, Small Icons, List, or Details.

Arrange icons on the Desktop

If your Desktop icons appear jumbled, or in an order other than what you expected, you can arrange them.

1 Use the right mouse button to click an empty area of the Desktop.

2 On the shortcut menu, point to Arrange Icons, and then click By Name.

The icons are arranged by name on your Desktop.

3 Use the right mouse button to click an empty area of the Desktop again.

4 On the shortcut menu, point to Arrange Icons, and then click Auto Arrange to arrange your icons.

Arrange icons in My Computer or Windows NT Explorer

If the icons in a My Computer window or in Windows NT Explorer appear jumbled, or in an order other than what you expected, you can arrange them. The icons can have a different arrangement for each window that you open.

1 In the My Computer or Windows NT Explorer window, click the View menu.

2 On the View menu, point to Arrange Icons, and then click By Name.

The icons are arranged by name in your window.

3 On the View menu, point to Arrange Icons again, and then click Auto Arrange.

Hide filename extensions in My Computer or Windows NT Explorer

If the filenames in My Computer or Windows NT Explorer include three-letter extensions, you can hide the extensions for file types that Windows NT Workstation recognizes. For example, Windows NT Workstation automatically recognizes file types with a .doc extension as being WordPad files.

1   In the My Computer or Windows NT Explorer window, click the View menu.

2   On the View menu, click Options.

3   On the Options dialog box, click the View tab, if necessary.

4   On the View tab, select the Hide MS-DOS Extensions For File Types That Are Registered check box.

5   Click OK.

Open cascading My Computer windows

You can set your display up so that a new My Computer window appears every time you open a new folder. You can also browse through folders using a single window that changes each time you open a new folder.

1   In the My Computer window, on the View menu, click Options.

2   In the Options dialog box, be sure that the Folder tab is active.

3   On the Folder tab, click the Browse Folders Using A Separate Window For Each Folder option button.

Working with Other Operating Systems

This appendix contains tips for moving from a previous version of Microsoft Windows or Windows NT Workstation to Microsoft Windows NT Workstation version 4.0. It also includes tips for working with MS-DOS programs in Windows NT.

Naming Files So That They Make Sense

Microsoft Windows NT Workstation version 4.0 allows you to use long filenames rather than the MS-DOS conventions, where filenames could be no longer than eight characters with a three-digit extension. If you need to use your Windows NT version 4.0 files with a previous version of Windows, Windows NT, or MS-DOS, be aware that the file name appears truncated in the older operating system. For example, if you named a file **Toys Marketing 1997.doc**, the filename will automatically appear shortened to **toysma~1.doc** in the older operating system. This may cause some confusion if you're sharing files with people who may be running a different operating system. In some cases, you may want to limit your file names to eight digits with a three-digit extension.

Likewise, if you have two long filenames that are almost identical, such as **Toys Marketing 1996.doc** and **Toys Marketing 1997.doc**. When the filenames appear in their truncated form, they will be **tosyma~1.doc** and **toysma~2.doc**. In order to tell which file is which, you or other people you're sharing the files with will have to open both documents, rather than just looking at the filenames.

TIP When you look at a directory list of files from within an MS-DOS window, you see the truncated version of the filename on the left side of the screen and the long filename appears immediately after the time the file was created. This is one way to quickly tell the difference between two files that have similar names and to prevent accidental deletion or overwriting.

Working with Older Windows, Windows NT, or MS-DOS Programs

Some of your programs may not run at all under Microsoft Windows NT version 4.0 because they were made for a previous version of Microsoft Windows, Microsoft Windows NT, or for MS-DOS. In other cases, you may be able to start a program only to find that it sometimes "hangs" after you begin working.

Close a program that isn't responding

When a program stops responding, you can use this procedure to close it. However, you will lose any changes you made to your document since the last time you saved it.

1 Press CTRL+ALT+DELETE.

The Windows NT Security dialog box appears.

2 Click the Task Manager button.

3 Click the name of the program you want to close.

4 Click the End Task button.

Microsoft Windows NT forces the program to end.

Close

5 Click the Close button.

Finding File Manager

In Microsoft Windows NT 4.0, File Manager has been replaced by My Computer and Windows NT Explorer. If you still want to use File Manager while you become accustomed to the new features in Windows NT version 4.0, you can add it to your Programs menu.

Add File Manger to your Programs menu

1 Click the Start button, point to Settings, and then click Taskbar.

2 Click the Start Menu Programs tab, and then click Add.

The Create Shortcut dialog box appears.

3 In the Command Line text box, type **winfile**, and then click Next.

4   Click the Programs icon if necessary, and then click Next.
5   In the text box, type File Manager, and then click Finish.
6   Click OK.

File Manager is added to the Programs menu on your Start menu.

accessories   Basic built-in programs included with Microsoft Windows NT, such as WordPad and Paint, that you can use to do your everyday work. Accessories also include utilities that help you use your computer's telecommunication, fax, and multimedia capabilities. System tools are accessories that help you manage your computer resources. Games are also included as part of your Windows NT accessories.

active window   In a multiple-window environment, the window that is currently selected and whose contents will be affected by all mouse actions, commands, and text entries.

application   *See* program.

arrow keys   The UP ARROW, DOWN ARROW, LEFT ARROW, and RIGHT ARROW keys that are used to move the insertion point or to select from a menu or a list of options.

back up   To create a duplicate copy of files to ensure against loss or damage.

backup disk   A disk that contains information copied from another disk or drive.

bit map   Typically, bit map refers to graphic images that are displayed on a computer screen. Bit map also refers to the file type .BMP, which is the default file type for the Paint accessory in Windows NT.

byte   The unit of measurement for information stored on a computer. In English, one character takes the space of one byte. The capacity of computer memory (RAM) and storage (disk space) are measured in bytes.

Calculator   The Microsoft Windows NT accessory you can use to perform numeric, scientific, or statistical calculations.

cascading menu   A menu that opens another menu. A cascading menu has a right-pointing arrow after its name, indicating that it opens another menu. For example, on the Start menu, the Programs command is followed by a right-pointing arrow, indicating that it opens another menu.

CD-ROM   A compact optical disk, similar in appearance to an audio CD, that can store over 500 MB of read-only information. A CD-ROM drive is need to read the data on a CD-ROM.

central processing unit (CPU)   The main processing component of a computer that interprets and carries out the directions of computer programs. The CPU directs the functions of input, output, and storage devices using the instructions defined by your computer programs.

Character Map   The Windows NT accessory that displays available characters in a selected font. It is most often used to insert special symbols into a document that are not easily typed from the keyboard.

Clipboard A temporary holding area in computer memory that stores the last set of information that was cut or copied (such as text or graphics). You transfer data from the Clipboard by using the Paste command. The information remains on the Clipboard until you cut or copy another piece of information, which then replaces the current contents of the Clipboard.

Close button The button in the upper-right corner of a Windows NT window that you click to close the window. Closing a program window exits the program.

command An instruction issued by a user that causes an action to be carried out by the computer program. You choose a command to start an activity, such as running a program, opening a document, or closing a file.

communication port Typically, an external connector at the back of a computer system that can be used to connect a modem, a printer, a scanner, a mouse, or another similar device. Communication ports have names, such as COM1 and COM2. *See also* port.

Control Panel The set of Windows NT programs that you can use to change system, hardware, software, and Windows NT settings.

copy To duplicate information from one location to another, either within a file, to another file, or to a file in another program. The copied information is stored on the Clipboard until you cut or copy another piece of information.

cut To remove selected information from a document so you can paste it to another location within the file, or to another file, or to a file in another program. The cut information is stored on the Clipboard until you cut or copy another piece of information.

data files The files that you create or modify using a program such as WordPad, Paint, Microsoft Word, or Microsoft Excel.

default A predefined setting that is built into a program and is used when you do not specify an alternative setting. For example, a document might have a default setting of one-inch page margins unless you specify another value for the margin settings.

Desktop The entire Windows NT screen that represents your work area. Icons, windows, and the taskbar appear on the Desktop. You can customize the Desktop to suit your preferences and working requirements.

destination A document or program receiving information that was originally generated in another program. *See also* source.

dialog box A type of window in which you can specify additional details for a command activity.

Dial-Up Networking   The Windows NT accessory you use to connect two computers that each have a modem. With Dial-Up Networking, you can share information between the two computers, even if the computers are not on a network.

disk   A round, flat piece of flexible plastic (floppy disk) or inflexible metal (hard disk) that stores data. The disk is coated with a magnetic material on which digital information can be recorded. To protect this material, disks are enclosed in plastic or metal casings.

disk drive   A hardware mechanism that reads information from a disk and writes information to a disk.

document   Any independent unit of information, such as a text file, worksheet, or graphic object, that is created with a program. A document can be saved with a unique filename by which it can be retrieved.

Documents menu   A cascading menu off the Windows NT Start menu that lists shortcuts to the last 15 document files you opened. When you click a document filename on the Documents menu, the program and the document open.

document window   A rectangular portion of the screen in which you view and edit a document. You can have multiple document windows open on the Desktop, and you can switch between windows using the taskbar.

drag-and-drop   A mouse technique for directly moving or copying a set of information from one location to another. To drag an object, position the pointer over the object, hold down the mouse button while you move the mouse, and then release the mouse button when the object is positioned where you want it.

drive   *See* disk drive.

edit   To add, delete, or change information, such as text or graphics.

electronic mail   Notes, messages, or files that are sent between different computers using telecommunication or network services. Also referred to as *e-mail*.

embed   To insert an object from a source program into a destination document. When you double-click the object in the destination document, the source program opens and you can edit the object. *See also* link.

file   A document that you create or save with a unique filename.

file type   The category designation of a file object. Files types include bit map, text, or spreadsheet. Windows NT automatically recognizes some file types such as bit map (.BMP), text (.TXT), or spreadsheet (.XLS), and displays an icon next to these recognized file types. Usually, different programs, such as Microsoft Word or Microsoft Excel have different file types.

folder   A container in which documents, program files, and other folders are stored on your computer disks. Folders can help you organize your documents by grouping them into categories, as you would organize paper documents into file folders. Formerly referred to as a *directory*.

font   A family of type styles, such as Times or Helvetica. Effects, such as bold or italic, are possible within one font, and various point sizes can be applied to a font.

format   The way text appears on a page. The four types of formats are character, paragraph, section, and document. Styles can be applied to any of these formats. Format can also refer to preparing a disk to record or retrieve data. Formatting usually erases any information previously stored on the disk.

full access   An attribute of a disk volume, folder, or file that is stored on a shared computer or network computer, and made available to other users on the network. Full access allows users to make any changes to the volume, folder, or file. *See also* read-only.

graphical user interface   A pictorial representation on a computer screen of the files, data, devices, and programs stored on the computer. A user can issue commands to the computer by interacting with the graphic images displayed on the screen.

hardware   The physical parts of a computer system, such as the monitor, keyboard, and printer.

HyperTerminal   The Windows NT accessory you can use to call another computer. HyperTerminal is especially useful when you want to log on to a bulletin board service, a remote computer or an online service.

icon   A small graphic that represents an object, such as a program, a disk drive, or a document. When you double-click an icon, the item the icon represents opens.

insertion point   The blinking vertical bar that marks the location where text is entered in a document or in a dialog box. You can move the insertion point by clicking the mouse in another location or by using the keyboard arrow keys.

link   To copy an object, such as a graphic or text, from one file or program to another so that there is a dependent relationship between the object and its source file. *Link* also refers to the connection between a source file and a destination file. Whenever the original information in the source file changes, the information in the linked object is automatically updated. *See also* embed.

map   To designate a shared computer, drive, or folder on a network computer as a drive available to your computer. When you map a folder or drive, you create a network drive on your computer through which you can use shared resources on the network computer.

Maximize button   The button in the upper-right corner of most windows that enlarges the window to fill the entire screen.

menu   A list of commands that can be executed using the mouse or keyboard shortcuts. For example, when you click the Start button on the Desktop, the Start menu appears.

microprocessor   The central processing chip in a personal computer. Common microprocessors for IBM and IBM-compatible computers include the Intel 386, 486, and Pentium chips.

Microsoft Exchange   The Windows NT program you can use to send and receive electronic mail, faxes, and files on a network or online service. Microsoft Exchange acts as a central "post office" for all messaging activities.

Minimize button   A button in the upper-right corner of most windows. When you click the Minimize button, the window is minimized to its button on the taskbar. The program and document remain open when a window is minimized.

modem   A hardware device that converts digital computer information into audio signals that can be sent through phone lines. These signals are received and converted back to digital signals by the receiving modem.

MS-DOS–based program   A program designed to run under the MS-DOS operating system.

My Briefcase   The Windows NT program you can use to store and synchronize duplicate sets of files and folders between two different computers.

My Computer   The Windows NT program that you can use to browse through your computer's filing system, and to open drives, folders, and files. You can also use My Computer to manage your files and your filing system, by moving, copying, renaming, and deleting items.

network   A system of multiple computers that uses special networking programs to share files, programs, printers, and other resources among the different computers that are connected to the network.

Network Neighborhood   The Windows NT program that you can use to explore the network to which your computer is connected.

OLE   A feature that allows you to import information from a source document into a destination document. The two options for OLE are linking and embedding. *See also* link *and* embed.

online service   A subscription computer service that you can use to call a computer and access information. You can obtain reports on news, sports, weather, the stock market and more. The Microsoft Network is an example of an online service.

Paint   The Windows NT accessory that you can use to create, edit, and view drawings.

password   A unique series of characters that you type to gain entry to the Windows NT network, your electronic mail, or a protected folder or file. Passwords are used to protect the security of a computer system and the private information stored on a computer.

paste   To insert cut or copied text from the temporary storage area, called the Clipboard, into a document.

path   The location of a file within a computer file system. The path indicates the filename preceded by the disk drive, folder, and subfolders in which the file is stored. If the file is on another computer on a network, the path also includes the computer name.

pixel   Short for "picture element." The smallest graphic unit that can be displayed on your screen. All the images displayed on a computer screen are composed of pixels. *See also* bit map.

port   A socket or slot that is a connector to your computer system unit into which you can plug the adapter for a hardware device, such as a printer, hard disk, modem, or mouse.

private folder   A folder stored on a shared, network computer that has not been designated as available to other users on the network. Only the user who created the folder can open, view, or edit the files in a private folder.

program   A computer software program, such as a word processor, spreadsheet, presentation designer, or relational database, that is designed to do a specific type of work.

read-only   An attribute of a disk volume, folder, or file stored on a shared, network computer that is made available to other users on the network. An item designated as read-only can be viewed by users, but not edited. *See also* full access.

Recycle Bin   The Windows NT program that holds files, folders, and other items you have deleted. Recycle Bin is represented by an icon on the Desktop. Until Recycle Bin is "emptied," you can recover items you have deleted or placed in Recycle Bin.

remote computer   A computer at another location that you can access on a network or through telecommunication by using your own, local computer.

Restore button   The button in the upper-right corner of a maximized window that restores the window from its maximized size back to its original size.

save   The function that stores information residing in memory into a designated place, under a designated name on one of your computer's disks.

scroll arrow   An arrow button that appears on either side of the scroll bar. You can use these arrow buttons to move the scroll box in either direction.

scroll bar   A band that appears along a window's right edge for vertical scrolling, or along the bottom edge for horizontal scrolling. Each scroll bar contains scroll arrows and a scroll box. When a scroll bar appears on your window, this indicates that you have more information in the window than is currently visible.

scroll box   The rectangle that appears inside the scroll bar. Its relative location on the scroll bar indicates the position of the window's visible contents relative to its total contents. You can drag the scroll box to scroll the window contents in larger increments than with the scroll arrows.

server   A central computer to which all computers on the network are connected, and through which users can obtain shared network resources.

shared resources   Hardware, software, or information that users on the network have identified as being available to others.

shortcut   An object that acts as a pointer to a document, folder, or program. If you double-click the shortcut, the object opens.

shortcut menu   A menu of commands that appears when you click the right mouse button while your mouse pointer is on a toolbar, control, or the Desktop, for example. The content of the menu varies based on the element you click.

source   The document or program in which the data was originally created. *See also* destination.

Start button   The command button in the lower-left corner of the Windows NT Desktop. The Start button serves as the starting point from which all Windows NT programs, activities, and functions begin.

Start menu   The menu that presents commands that are a starting point for all work you do on your computer, such as starting a program, opening a document, finding a file, and getting help. You open the Start menu by clicking the Start button displayed on the Desktop.

status bar   A bar at the bottom of the screen that displays information about the currently selected command, the active dialog box, the standard keys on the keyboard, or the current state of the program and the keyboard. You can turn the display of the status bar off and on.

system administrator   The person who sets up and maintains the network. The system administrator can grant or deny access permission to files, folders, and printers to other members in a workgroup. Your system administrator can also answer questions you may have about your organization's network.

tab dialog box   A type of dialog box divided into two or more categories, which can be accessed by clicking the named tabs at the top of the dialog box. *See also* dialog box.

taskbar   The rectangular bar usually located across the bottom of the Windows NT Desktop. The taskbar includes the Start button as well as buttons for any programs and documents that are open. Its location, size, and visibility can be modified to fit your preferences.

telecommunication   The technology for using your computer, modem, and phone lines to communicate with other computers and users.

title bar   The horizontal bar at the top of a window that displays the name of the document or program that appears in that window.

toolbar   A bar at the top of Windows-based programs that display a set of buttons used to carry out common menu commands. The buttons displayed on a toolbar change depending on which window or view is currently selected.

window   A rectangular, bordered element on the Windows NT screen. You can have multiple windows open at the same time on your Desktop, with each window running a different program or displaying a different document.

Windows NT-based program   A program designed to run under the Windows NT operating system. *See also* MS-DOS–based programs.

Windows NT Explorer   The Windows NT program you can use to browse through, open, and manage the disk drives, folders, and files on your computer. You can also use Windows NT Explorer to view and open shared folders on other computers on the network. You can use Windows NT Explorer to manage your files and your filing system by moving, copying, renaming, and deleting files.

WordPad   The Windows NT accessory you can use to create, edit, format, and view short text documents.

Index

Everything you **need** for the **long run.**

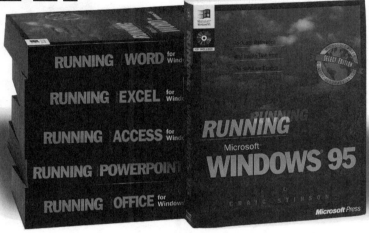

The *Running* series from Microsoft Press gives you comprehensive reference information and expert, friendly instruction, whether you're a new, an intermediate, or an advanced user. With complete guides to Microsoft® Windows® 95 and each of the robust Office applications, the *Running* series provides everything you need to get where you're going with a running start. The Microsoft Press® *Running* series is available at your favorite bookstore or software store. Run over there first.

Running Microsoft® Windows® 95
U.S.A. $29.95 ($39.95 Canada)
ISBN 1-55615-674-X

Running Microsoft® Word for Windows® 95
U.S.A. $29.95 ($39.95 Canada)
ISBN 1-55615-848-3

Running Microsoft® Excel for Windows® 95
U.S.A. $29.95 ($39.95 Canada)
ISBN 1-55615-831-9

Running Microsoft® Access for Windows® 95
U.S.A. $39.95 ($53.95 Canada)
ISBN 1-55615-886-6

Running Microsoft® PowerPoint® for Windows® 95
U.S.A. $24.95 ($33.95 Canada)
ISBN 1-55615-852-1

Running Microsoft® Office for Windows® 95
U.S.A. $29.95 ($39.95 Canada)
ISBN 1-55615-897-1

Microsoft Press

Sure-footed training.

Just starting out with Microsoft® Office 95? Upgrading from an earlier version? Whichever, it's a smart idea to take everything new that you learn a careful step at a time. That is to say, rely on the Microsoft Press® *Step by Step* series. *Step by Step* books are self-paced, so you learn at the rate that's most comfortable for you. Because the training you get is tailored to your specific needs, you can put it to work right away. And you can always be sure the information in every *Step by Step* book is up-to-the-minute, complete, and authoritative. They're at your favorite bookstore or software store—from Microsoft Press. Nobody knows better how to get you where you want to go, step by step.

Upgrading to Microsoft® Windows® 95 Step by Step
U.S.A. $19.95   ($26.95 Canada)
ISBN 1-55615-816-5

Microsoft® Windows® 95 Step by Step
U.S.A. $29.95   ($39.95 Canada)
ISBN 1-55615-683-9

Microsoft® PowerPoint® for Windows® 95 Step by Step
U.S.A. $29.95   ($39.95 Canada)
ISBN 1-55615-829-7

Microsoft® Excel for Windows® 95 Step by Step
U.S.A. $29.95   ($39.95 Canada)
ISBN 1-55615-825-4

Microsoft® Office 95 Integration Step by Step
U.S.A. $29.95   ($39.95 Canada)
ISBN 1-55615-887-4

Microsoft® Access for Windows® 95 Step by Step
U.S.A. $29.95   ($39.95 Canada)
ISBN 1-55615-876-9

Microsoft® Word for Windows® 95 Step by Step
U.S.A. $29.95   ($39.95 Canada)
ISBN 1-55615-828-9

Microsoft·Press

Microsoft Press® books are available wherever quality books are sold, and through CompuServe's Electronic Mall—**GO MSP**—or our Web page, http://www.microsoft.com/mspress/. Call **1-800-MSPRESS** for more information or to place a credit card order.* Please refer to **BBK** when placing your order. Prices subject to change.

*In Canada, contact Macmillan Canada, Attn: Microsoft Press Dept., 164 Commander Blvd., Agincourt, Ontario, Canada M1S 3C7, or call 1-800-667-1115. Outside the U.S. and Canada, write to International Coordinator, Microsoft Press, One Microsoft Way, Redmond, WA 98052-6399, or fax +1-206-936-7329.

IMPORTANT — READ CAREFULLY BEFORE OPENING SOFTWARE PACKET(S).
By opening the sealed packet(s) containing the software, you indicate your acceptance
of the following Microsoft License Agreement.

Microsoft License Agreement

MICROSOFT LICENSE AGREEMENT
(Single User Products)

This is a legal agreement between you (either an individual or an entity) and Microsoft Corporation. By opening the sealed software packet(s) you are agreeing to be bound by the terms of this agreement. If you do not agree to the terms of this agreement, promptly return the book, including the unopened software packet(s), to the place you obtained it for a full refund.

MICROSOFT SOFTWARE LICENSE

1. GRANT OF LICENSE. Microsoft grants to you the right to use one copy of the Microsoft software program included with this book (the "SOFTWARE") on a single terminal connected to a single computer. The SOFTWARE is in "use" on a computer when it is loaded into temporary memory (i.e., RAM) or installed into permanent memory (e.g., hard disk, CD-ROM, or other storage device) of that computer. You may not network the SOFTWARE or otherwise use it on more than one computer or computer terminal at the same time.

2. COPYRIGHT. The SOFTWARE is owned by Microsoft or its suppliers and is protected by United States copyright laws and international treaty provisions. Therefore, you must treat the SOFTWARE like any other copyrighted material (e.g., a book or musical recording) except that you may either (a) make one copy of the SOFTWARE solely for backup or archival purposes, or (b) transfer the SOFTWARE to a single hard disk provided you keep the original solely for backup or archival purposes. You may not copy the written materials accompanying the SOFTWARE.

3. OTHER RESTRICTIONS. You may not rent or lease the SOFTWARE, but you may transfer the SOFTWARE and accompanying written materials on a permanent basis provided you retain no copies and the recipient agrees to the terms of this Agreement. You may not reverse engineer, decompile, or disassemble the SOFTWARE. If the SOFTWARE is an update or has been updated, any transfer must include the most recent update and all prior versions.

4. DUAL MEDIA SOFTWARE. If the SOFTWARE package contains both 3.5" and 5.25" disks, then you may use only the disks appropriate for your single-user computer. You may not use the other disks on another computer or loan, rent, lease, or transfer them to another user except as part of the permanent transfer (as provided above) of all SOFTWARE and written materials.

5. LANGUAGE SOFTWARE. If the SOFTWARE is a Microsoft language product, then you have a royalty-free right to reproduce and distribute executable files created using the SOFTWARE. If the language product is a Basic or COBOL product, then Microsoft grants you a royalty-free right to reproduce and distribute the run-time modules of the SOFTWARE provided that you: (a) distribute the run-time modules only in conjunction with and as a part of your software product; (b) do not use Microsoft's name, logo, or trademarks to market your software product; (c) include a valid copyright notice on your software product; and (d) agree to indemnify, hold harmless, and defend Microsoft and its suppliers from and against any claims or lawsuits, including attorneys' fees, that arise or result from the use or distribution of your software product. The "run-time modules" are those files in the SOFTWARE that are identified in the accompanying written materials as required during execution of your software program. The run-time modules are limited to run-time files, install files, and ISAM and REBUILD files. If required in the SOFTWARE documentation, you agree to display the designated patent notices on the packaging and in the README file of your software product.

LIMITED WARRANTY

LIMITED WARRANTY. Microsoft warrants that (a) the SOFTWARE will perform substantially in accordance with the accompanying written materials for a period of ninety (90) days from the date of receipt, and (b) any hardware accompanying the SOFTWARE will be free from defects in materials and workmanship under normal use and service for a period of one (1) year from the date of receipt. Any implied warranties on the SOFTWARE and hardware are limited to ninety (90) days and one (1) year, respectively. Some states/countries do not allow limitations on duration of an implied warranty, so the above limitation may not apply to you.

CUSTOMER REMEDIES. Microsoft's and its suppliers' entire liability and your exclusive remedy shall be, at Microsoft's option, either (a) return of the price paid, or (b) repair or replacement of the SOFTWARE or hardware that does not meet Microsoft's Limited Warranty and which is returned to Microsoft with a copy of your receipt. This Limited Warranty is void if failure of the SOFTWARE or hardware has resulted from accident, abuse, or misapplication. Any replacement SOFTWARE or hardware will be warranted for the remainder of the original warranty period or thirty (30) days, whichever is longer. Outside the United States, these remedies are not available without proof of purchase from an authorized non-U.S. source.

NO OTHER WARRANTIES. Microsoft and its suppliers disclaim all other warranties, either express or implied, including, but not limited to implied warranties of merchantability and fitness for a particular purpose, with regard to the SOFTWARE, the accompanying written materials, and any accompanying hardware. This limited warranty gives you specific legal rights. You may have others which vary from state/country to state/country.

NO LIABILITY FOR CONSEQUENTIAL DAMAGES. In no event shall Microsoft or its suppliers be liable for any damages whatsoever (including without limitation, damages for loss of business profits, business interruption, loss of business information, or any other pecuniary loss) arising out of the use of or inability to use this Microsoft product, even if Microsoft has been advised of the possibility of such damages. Because some states/countries do not allow the exclusion or limitation of liability for consequential or incidental damages, the above limitation may not apply to you.

U.S. GOVERNMENT RESTRICTED RIGHTS

The SOFTWARE and documentation are provided with RESTRICTED RIGHTS. Use, duplication, or disclosure by the Government is subject to restrictions as set forth in subparagraph (c)(1)(ii) of The Rights in Technical Data and Computer Software clause at DFARS 252.227-7013 or subparagraphs (c)(1) and (2) of the Commercial Computer Software — Restricted Rights 48 CFR 52.227-19, as applicable. Manufacturer is Microsoft Corporation, One Microsoft Way, Redmond, WA 98052-6399.

This Agreement is governed by the laws of the State of Washington.

Should you have any questions concerning this Agreement, or if you desire to contact Microsoft for any reason, please write: Microsoft Sales and Service, One Microsoft Way, Redmond, WA 98052-6399.

The
Step by Step
Practice Files Disk

The enclosed 3.5-inch disk contains timesaving, ready-to-use practice files that complement the lessons in this book. To use the practice files, you'll need Windows NT Workstation version 4.0.

Each *Step by Step* lesson uses practice files from the disk. Before you begin the *Step by Step* lessons, read the "Installing and Using the Practice Files" section of the book for easy instructions telling how to install the files on your computer's hard disk. As you work through each lesson, be sure to follow the instructions for renaming the practice files so that you can go through a lesson more than once if you need to.

Please take a few moments to read the License Agreement on the previous page before using the enclosed disk.

Register your Microsoft Press® book today, and let us know what you think.

At Microsoft Press, we listen to our customers. We update our books as new releases of software are issued, and we'd like you to tell us the kinds of additional information you'd find most useful in these updates. Your feedback will be considered when we prepare a future edition; plus, when you become a registered owner, you will get Microsoft Press catalogs and exclusive offers on specially priced books.
Thanks!

I used this book as
- ● A way to learn the software
- ● A reference when I needed it
- ● A way to find out about advanced features
- ● Other_____

I consider myself
- ● A beginner or an occasional computer user
- ● An intermediate-level user with a pretty good grasp of the basics
- ● An advanced user who helps and provides solutions for others
- ● Other_____

I purchased this book from
- ● A bookstore
- ● A software store
- ● A direct mail offer
- ● Other_____

I will buy the next edition of the book when it's updated
- ● Definitely
- ● Probably
- ● I will not buy the next edition

The next edition of this book should include the following additional information:
1•_____
2•_____
3•_____

The most useful things about this book are_____

This book would be more helpful if_____

My general impressions of this book are_____

May we contact you regarding your comments? ● Yes ● No
Would you like to receive Microsoft Press catalogs regularly? ● Yes ● No

Name_____
Company (if applicable)_____
Address_____
City_____State_____Zip_____
Daytime phone number (optional) (_____)_____

Please mail back your feedback form—postage free! Fold this form as
described on the other side of this card, or fax this sheet to:
Microsoft Press, Attn: Marketing Department, fax 206-936-7329

NO POSTAGE
NECESSARY
IF MAILED
IN THE
UNITED STATES

BUSINESS REPLY MAIL
FIRST-CLASS MAIL   PERMIT NO. 108   REDMOND, WA

POSTAGE WILL BE PAID BY ADDRESSEE

MICROSOFT PRESS
ONE MICROSOFT WAY
REDMOND WA 98052-9953

FOLD HERE